"A few nights ago my boys wanted *Adventures Around Cincinnati* for their bedtime book. They loved hearing about all the places we have visited in detail, especially if they involve trains. I love visiting places that I never knew about even after living in this area my entire life." –Pam Peebles

"So many things I would never have found by myself. Cincinnati has a ferry!?! The handy table in the back helps me find the perfect Adventure and I can take notes on the extra pages. Laura and Terri thought of everything!" –Tellina Addison

"Love how this book is bringing families together all around the city! *Adventures Around Cincinnati* is just what we need in this fast-paced world.... it encourages families to take some time for each other and make wonderful memories!! Keep up the great work!" –Jennie and Kim, motherhoodsupport.com

"*Adventures Around Cincinnati* offers a wealth of ideas and information perfect for any southern Ohio parent, grandparent, teacher, newcomer, or tourist. I've lived in the area for over 16 years and discovered gems I had never heard of listed in this book." –Sharon Siepel, author of *Essential Survival Guide to Living on Your Own*

"After hearing Laura and Terri speak about *Adventures Around Cincinnati*, I knew this was my summer survival answer. We planned our weekly trips and were instantly hooked. I scrapbooked each Adventure and ended up with a beautiful album. *Adventures Around Cincinnati* has helped me create a new family tradition and memories with my children that we will all cherish forever!" –Jeanne Dwyer

"What is super neat about this book is it helps you connect with not just your kids, but your BOYS on a higher level... men build relationships by DOING stuff. This is the best of Cincinnati for families, all rolled into one convenient location. It also helps build relationship with other women, or your husband, as it's always good to do these with another adult, if you want the company. It's also a great resource for when family comes to visit—we always send visitors a copy of the book before they arrive!" –Nina Roesner, author of *The Respect Dare*

"Love this book! It's got all the info I want and not all the 'fillers' I don't! Love the help with age ranges; helps me know which attractions to take my little guys to and which ones to save for a little later. My friend and I are planning to do a monthly Adventure with our kiddos; we're tie-dying our matching T-shirts tomorrow to get started!" –Allison Dumont

"When our company transfers someone to the Greater Cincinnati area, I sometimes sense a little trepidation. They are afraid Cincinnati will be a little 'sleepy' compared to the other parts of the world from which they come. I give every one of them a copy of *Adventures Around Cincinnati*. This book quickly shows them that Cincinnati is a deeply vibrant city full of exciting activities for adults, children, and families. It is an invaluable resource for new arrivals!" –Rob Ratterman, Founder, CanDo.com

"We had an Adventure every week this year; we made tons of memories and learned a lot. My copy is already dog-eared after six months because we use it so much." –Christy Mose

"This book has been VERY helpful for inspiring memorable outings for our home school group!" –Jennifer Conn

"There is nothing worse than sitting around all summer with two boys not knowing what to do. That's when I open up my *Adventures Around Cincinnati* book and can easily get my creative juices flowing and find something fun for all of us." –Tonya Oriol

"This little book is a treasure. Within its pages are so many fun ideas of how to create memories with our families and friends! In a world that challenges us to retain sacred moments of slowing down and embracing carefree timelessness, this book is a refreshing reminder that life isn't meant to be lived at full throttle all the time. Thanks, *Adventures Around Cincinnati*, for reminding us to 'take time to smell the roses.' Keep a copy handy in your car for quick reference! Also makes a great 'welcome' gift to someone new to the area, a unique teacher or coach's gift, or a special way of saying thank you to a friend or neighbor." –Mary Martin

"The book you have in your hands is valuable whether you have lived in Greater Cincinnati all of your life (like me), or if you are planning a vacation or a family visit. This is a great memory-making tool for families because it provides accurate information on the most enjoyable places this region has to offer. While reading the book, I reflected on happy memories from my own childhood as well as the smiles on my own children's faces when I took them to some of these places. Enjoy reading this book and start making new memories now. You won't find a better guide available." –Bradford S. Summers, Ph.D., Psychotherapist in Private Practice

ADVENTURES Around CINCINNATI

A Parent's Guide to Unique and Memorable Places to Explore with your Kids

ADVENTURES
... Around ...
CINCINNATI

A Parent's Guide to Unique and Memorable Places to Explore with your Kids

LAURA HOEVENER and TERRI WEEKS

Hourglass Press
Milford, OH

Hourglass Press
Milford, OH
www.hourglasspress.net

Disclaimer: All recreational activities include a certain amount of risk. The publisher and authors disclaim any responsibility and any liability for any injury, harm, or illness that may occur through or by use of any information in this book.

Although every attempt was made to ensure the information contained in this book was accurate at time of printing, prices, hours, and availability of any of the destinations listed may change at any given time. The publisher and authors assume no responsibility for errors or inaccuracies. Any slights against any entries or organizations are unintentional.

Trademarked names, including names of destinations, are used in this book in an editorial context with no intention of infringement of the trademark.

All Scripture quotations in this publication are from the Contemporary English Version Copyright © 1991, 1992, 1995 by American Bible Society, used by Permission.

ISBN-13 - 978-0-9910854-0-8
LCCN - 2013956295

Cover Design by Alan Pranke
Cover photography by Tim Jeffries, Terri Weeks, and Laura Hoevener
Typeset by Melanie Shellito
Maps by Kim Jorden
Edited by Paula Goodnight, Where's My Pen? Copywriting and Editing Services

To buy books in quantity or schedule a speaking engagement, contact the authors.

Email: contactus@adventuresaroundcincinnati.com
Website: www.adventuresaroundcincinnati.com
Facebook: Adventures Around Cincinnati
Twitter: AdventureCincy

Printed in the United States of America

ACKNOWLEDGMENTS

Laura would like to thank:

My wonderful husband John, for providing advice and being supportive of my many hours working on this project; my children, Daniel, Anna, and Morgan, for being willing and cheerful Adventurers; Terri, for being a great friend, co-author, and committed Adventure partner; my friends and family, for supporting me and praying for me on this book writing Adventure; and my mom, for always being there for me. Thanks to my adventurous sister-in-law, Amber, for spending many hours with my kids so I could focus on writing. I couldn't have written this book without the support and encouragement from all of you!

Terri would like to thank:

My amazing husband Curtis, for your unwaivering support through two editions of this book; my children, Connor, Corinne, and Camille, for your enthusiasm about our Adventures and this book; Laura, for your friendship, your Adventure Tuesday partnership, and for getting us started on the speaking and writing journey; and my parents, family, and friends, who have encouraged me along the way. You are all precious to me.

Both of us would like to thank:

Paula Goodnight of Where's My Pen? Copywriting and Editing Services, for your many hours of work on this project and all your helpful advice; Kim Jorden, for your many hours of work drawing and revising our maps; Nina Roesner of Greater Impact Ministries, for mentoring us along our book-writing journey; Connie Hammer and Tim Jeffries, for the photography; Sharon Siepel, for all your support and encouragement; Joni Sullivan Baker of Buoyancy Public Relations, for your guidance and help; Tracey Johnson and everyone behind the scenes at FOX19 Cincinnati, for giving us time every month to share new Adventures with your viewers. A huge thank you to our advisory team for all your input: Alicia, Amber, Angela, Christy, Daniel, Heather, Kimberly, Kristen, Laura, Leah, Mary, Neila, Rhonda, Shea, Tonya, and Vickie. A million thanks to our readers and fans for your suggestions, your enthusiasm, and your dedication to Adventures—it has meant more than you will ever know. Lastly, we thank God, our provider, for the inspiration to write this book and His help along the way.

TABLE OF CONTENTS

INTRODUCTION

As a parent, grandparent, caregiver, or anyone involved in the lives of children, you want to make the most of the days you spend with them. Wouldn't it be satisfying to plan a summer or a year full of new and different activities your children will enjoy? Do you want to create traditions they recall with fondness someday? This book encourages you to be intentional about having fun and creating memories while exploring your surroundings with your kids. It supplies a wide variety of suggested attractions, while also providing practical planning tips.

Since the first edition of this book was released in 2010, we have continued to discover more new Adventures with our kids. This second edition contains about 50 new Adventures that we recommend. We've also had the opportunity to speak to dozens of groups all over Greater Cincinnati and Dayton to share our story and discuss the attractions in our book, and to share Adventure ideas with the viewers of the FOX19 Morning Xtra Show every month. We've also released two ebooks. *The Totally Free Summer Staycation* is a companion to this book and contains a week's worth of Adventures that have no admission fees. *Adventures Around You* is geared for readers in cities other than Cincinnati. It explains benefits and tips for planning Adventures wherever home may be.

We are moms, and we know what it is like to have kids at home. Moms and dads need to cook meals, wash laundry, scrub bathrooms, and entertain kids. Even with all the work involved, it is important to carve out some recreational time to spend with your kids. If you schedule this time and are proactive about making plans, you are rewarded with some precious experiences that are imprinted forever in the minds of you and your children.

We started writing the first edition of this book after six years of planning weekly summer "Adventures," as we call them, with our kids. Since its inception, our Adventures have brought us many priceless moments with our children and gave us the chance to see new experiences through their eyes. These weekly excursions are a part of our identity and have created a tradition that our kids won't let us bring to an end! We found some amusing, unique, and educational locations, each one adding another page to the scrapbook of our children's lives. With each Adventure, we explore the area around us, learn something new, and enjoy each other's company. Many attractions are open year round, and if you can fit them into your schedule, you won't regret it. We have planned Adventures over spring break, on weekends, and on school holidays. Summer break, though, has been our best opportunity for weekly plans and squeezing all we can out of the kids' school vacation.

Of course, there are other ways to use this book. We realize not everyone is a stay-at-home parent nor has summers off. You could also plan monthly Adventures on weekends that include your spouse, or use this book to arrange a "staycation" (stay-at-home vacation). Another option is to find something refreshing to do with out-of-town guests or plan a lively weekend trip with your family. Homeschooling families may plan field trips fitting in with their current area of study.

Parents don't have a lot of time to read a long book, so we've made this concise and easy-to-follow. Do you want to have Adventures with the kids in your life? If your answer is yes, then read on as we explain exactly how we make this tradition with our kids so special.

What is an Adventure?

We define an Adventure as a planned outing on a day we set aside to explore a new destination with our kids. That day on our calendar is considered off-limits for scheduling other activities. An Adventure location might be scenic, entertaining, or educational. We generally keep the cost low, too. Any new and interesting site becomes the setting of another Adventure. Kids are happy doing simple things, like climbing the steps up and down the Serpentine Wall at Sawyer Point. They also enjoy structured activities such as attending a field trip with several friends at the airport. We found that planning activities is one of the keys to success. Without a plan, it's easy to let great ideas become forgotten and undone. This book helps you be intentional about making the most of the time that you have together.

When you take a vacation, do you study the travel brochures and try to squeeze in as many activities as possible? When you're away from home, it seems there are so many interesting things to see and places to go. Well, with an "Adventures" mindset, you end up finding fascinating places right in your own backyard. When you become a hometown tourist, you'll be amazed at all the entertaining destinations waiting to be discovered.

In Part One of this book, we share our experiences and give advice on how to plan and execute your own Adventures.

Part Two is a listing of kid-tested attractions within a two-hour drive from Cincinnati. In order to make it user-friendly for parents, we've included features like age recommendations and stroller-friendliness, so you can plan Adventures suited to your own family's needs.

Part Three organizes the attractions into different

categories to help you plan. Do you want to visit a museum? Look it up on our easy-to-use Adventure Table. Do your kids love animals? It's on the table, too. We hope this table will help you quickly find an outing that matches your interests. We've also included sample itineraries for summer and year-round Adventures, for readers who want to get a quick start with limited planning.

Part One

CREATING MEMORIES
WITH YOUR FAMILY

WHY ADVENTURES?

The Birth of Summer Adventures

It was the summer of 2003 and we had scheduled an outing with some friends at Parky's Farm at Winton Woods. We had recently invited a speaker to our MOPS (Mothers of Preschoolers) group to talk about the many fascinating destinations in the state of Ohio. We were both avid sightseers when living in other states, but had been unfamiliar with much of what Cincinnati had to offer. We were inspired to visit the many attractions, but overwhelmed with figuring out how to make it a reality. While at the park, we talked about trying to get together on a regular basis with our kids to explore our city as tourists would. We realized we would have to be deliberate about it. We picked a day that worked each week for both of us, made a commitment to each other to keep that day available, and our Summer Adventures were born!

That first summer was full of joy, learning, and some challenges, too. Our babies weren't even a year old yet. Besides the babies, together we had three other children under the age of five. We were still dealing with diapers, naptimes, nursing, sippy cups, and an occasional temper tantrum. It certainly wasn't always easy, but it was unforgettable. As our kids have gotten older, our Adventures have evolved. We can now travel farther, plan longer days, and even be riskier in our choices. What we've learned is that outings can be tailored to children of any age and to any kind of family. Even infants can travel along. Our daughters, Anna and Camille, think it's neat they've been going on Adventures for as long as they can remember. Morgan, the youngest in our crew, went on her first Adventure when she was just three weeks old!

Our Kids Love Adventures!

We started weekly Summer Adventures in 2003 and haven't stopped yet because our kids love them! As soon as the weather starts warming up in the spring, they start asking about the upcoming summer's Adventures. When we first started speaking to different groups and venues about our Adventures, we asked our kids for their thoughts regarding our summer Adventures. We heard some very positive answers. They like the excitement of new experiences. Terri's oldest daughter Corinne thinks it's cool to have opportunities like petting a shark at the Newport Aquarium. They like to remember past Adventures and talk about their favorites. They like to explore new places and spend time with their friends. Terri's son Connor said that it makes history interesting and fun.

Each year, Laura's son Daniel requests to go blueberry picking. He has great memories of this, and each year, per his request, we do it again. Was this our favorite? Well, here's the story: It was the summer of 2003, our first year of Adventures. Blueberry picking sounded like a great family activity. We envisioned children happily picking berries, a nice picnic lunch, and perhaps working together to bake a yummy pie or cobbler for dessert. The day was uncomfortably hot and sticky. As we walked with our berry buckets in hand, our two oldest boys (ages three and four at the time) were challenging each other to a berry picking competition. This battle never slowed down.

"I have the most berries of the kids!"

"No, I have the most berries!"

"NO, I do!"

"NO, I DO!"

This seemed to go on and on...and on and on. Now

remember, it was REALLY hot and muggy. On the bright side, there were plump, ripe berries everywhere, and we all felt compelled to keep picking. Pretty soon my (Laura's) baby started to fuss and nursing was the only thing that was going to make her happy. With nowhere to sit down, I stood in front of a blueberry bush, holding a nursing baby with one hand and picking blueberries with the other. I wasn't about to let those kids pick more blueberries than I did! All in all, it was a hot, sticky, miserable day, but we keep doing it again and again each year. Each year it's always my son's favorite Adventure. To top things off we take home some delicious berries to enjoy.

HOW CAN ADVENTURES BENEFIT YOUR FAMILY?

Memories for a Lifetime

There are so many benefits that come from Adventures it is hard to know where to begin. The most long-lasting benefit is the priceless memories you create that are cherished for the rest of your lives. Make sure to take your camera along to document your Adventures. Half of the fun is reliving them with your kids when you look back at the pictures. If you like to scrapbook, get ready for some extra work. All of your new excursions will provide plenty of material for some terrific scrapbook pages!

A Tradition to Remember

We've been planning Adventures for so long our kids assume these will always be a part of their summer plans. In fact, our crew doesn't remember a summer without them. They look forward to seeing their friends each week and experiencing something out of the ordinary. It has become a part of who we are as a family. Having a tradition like this makes your kids feel like they are a part of something special. As the parents and planners, we look forward to scheduling our summers and anticipating the experiences we will have. After over ten years, we still have a list of places we haven't yet visited and plan on continuing our Adventures through our kids' teen years. We are having too much fun to let Adventures end.

A Family that Plays Together, Stays Together

In his book, *Keep the Siblings, Lose the Rivalry*, Dr. Todd Cartmell says, "The amount of positive family bonding time you spend together with your children will have a direct impact on the quality of their relationships (with each other) when you're not around." So, if kids are having fun with each other, they will actually get along better the rest of the time. Being intentional about planning recreational time together really helps your kids interact more positively with each other! It can also be gratifying to give your family shared experiences to remember together.

Prepare Kids for Challenges

When we look at the values that we want to instill in our kids, we can see how these Adventures are shaping them. According to Licensed Professional Clinical Counselor Bill Ramsey, exposing children to different experiences and hands-on learning opportunities stimulates their brains in an important way. Their experiences form the foundation of their belief systems that determine how they deal with challenges for the rest of their lives. Exposure to a wide range of experiences helps them to think broadly and opens their minds to more possibilities.

Expand your Comfort Zone

We found that planning different Adventures each week requires us to get out of our comfort zones. Going to the pool every week or choosing a favorite park to visit would be easier than constantly finding new activities. Our hope as parents is that our children will develop a view that new experiences are exciting rather than scary. If they are at ease with the idea of leaving their comfort zones, then they will be better equipped as adults to face the unknown.

The Confidence Builder

Taking our kids on Adventures has given us the experience and confidence to plan longer Adventures and family vacations that allow us to see other parts of the country and world. Several years ago we attempted our first overnight Adventure. A low-cost airline was offering a deal we couldn't pass up, so we flew to Kansas City for an overnight trip. Late-night flights made it challenging, but it was a trip that none of us will forget. Several years ago, Terri's family made a goal to visit all 50 states. They also took a month-long trip to Scandinavia. While there, Terri even took her kids to two countries on her own after her husband returned to the US. This might have been very unnerving without the confidence gained through our Adventures. What might have seemed impossible a few years ago starts looking more feasible as you gain more experience.

Bill Ramsey also attests that Adventures build kids' confidence, especially if you are able to return to some of your favorite places. The first time they visit a place, they explore it. The second time they begin to take control and organize ideas. If you continue to return to a favorite spot, eventually the kids start feeling like experts. Although we advocate seeing new places, there are some solid reasons to make repeated visits to favorite locations, especially if your kids request it. On that note, while we generally try to plan new Adventures, we do sometimes repeat one. We have decided sometimes we all enjoy a destination so much it's worth experiencing again. Others we have revisited because the younger kids were too young to remember or because the older ones will now be able to see it with more mature eyes.

Adding Structure

From a practical standpoint, having a weekly routine that includes Adventures and other regular activities provides some needed structure in kids' summer schedules. Kids manage their emotions better when they know what to expect. My (Terri's) kids know that we do laundry on Monday, go on an Adventure on Tuesday, go to the library on Wednesday, and go shopping and run errands on Thursday.

Knowing that Adventures happen on Tuesday is also good for my (Laura's) family. We start the week off looking forward to Tuesday, and then the rest of the week can be spent doing whatever else needs to be done. The structure helps me to plan the tasks I need to accomplish during the week knowing that one day is unavailable. If I didn't have a planned day for an Adventure, it might never happen. Something more urgent might take priority and we'd probably put off our Adventure until the next week. Some structure can be a very good thing!

Take Some Risks, Reap the Rewards

When we plan our summers, we always put a few sure-fire winners into the schedule, but also take a risk or two and add some unknowns into the mix. For example, when we took a tour of the St. Mary's Cathedral Basilica of the

Assumption, we weren't sure how it would go over with the kids. But we knew that even if the kids hated it, we could assure them something better was planned for the next week. We can also stop at the park or treat the kids to ice cream afterwards to end a not-so-fun Adventure on a positive note. Since we know we can fit about nine Adventures into a summer, we can afford to take a few risks. We have had some rewarding and interesting experiences by taking these risks!

Accountability Makes All the Difference

We both knew we wanted to explore our region and be intentional about having fun and making memories with our kids. We also both knew we'd be more disciplined if we could commit to doing this with a friend. Accountability makes all the difference. If you make plans with someone who is expecting you to be there, it's a hard commitment to break. For instance, it would be easy to put off your own plans because you don't feel like packing a lunch, it might rain, or there is too much laundry to do. Knowing someone is counting on you helps you put the laundry off until the next day.

One summer, there was one week we both were extremely busy. There was no reason we should have tried to fit an Adventure into our crazy schedules. Between the two of us, we had kids in swim lessons and in day camp, there were out-of-town visitors, a nephew being born, a camping trip to pack for and a vacation that was about to begin. We each knew the other person was counting on us, so we went ahead with our plans. It may not have been the smartest thing we've ever done, but it proves that with advanced planning and accountability, you can make anything happen.

That's What Friends are For

Through our Adventures together, we have deepened our friendship over the years. In addition to the shared memories, we have had many conversations. We usually ride in one minivan and chat while we're driving. One of the most common responses we've heard after speaking to a group is, "I wish I had a friend like that." We want to encourage you that you can build a friendship like this and it's one of the many benefits of Adventures. Occasionally we wish our husbands could join us, but we know spending time with a girlfriend is also healthy for our marriages. You can certainly attempt Adventures by yourself, but they will be more enjoyable and memorable for the both the parent and the kids when you experience them with friends.

Sharing your Knowledge and Experience

Another benefit of Adventures is when you have out-of-town visitors, you can take them somewhere unique. They will think you are an expert on your hometown! Most out-of-town visitors will have heard of Kings Island. We love Kings Island, too, but we can help our visitors stretch their money further by telling them of many other options. Some of the kids' grandparents have joined us for an Adventure. Terri's mother-in-law drove all the way from Wisconsin because she said they sounded like so much fun she wanted to experience one herself. An Adventure lifestyle is contagious! It makes us smile to think when our kids have their own families they will be able to pass down to their kids their memories of going on exciting Adventures. Hopefully, someday we will be the grandmothers tagging along on our children's Adventures with our grandchildren.

Mission Accomplished

We have found that at the end of the summer, we can look back with a great sense of accomplishment. Sure, there are always activities we didn't complete, but when we take an inventory of the new and interesting places we have been, we don't have any regrets about how we spent our days. It's a great feeling to know you've made every effort to make it memorable. We look forward to planning our next summer almost as soon as the last Adventure has ended.

PLANNING AND EXECUTING YOUR OWN ADVENTURES

So you've decided that it would be a great idea to start adding Adventures into your routine. What are the next steps? We've put together some ideas to help you make this a reality. We have included numerous planning tips to think about before you head out on your first Adventure. This chapter contains all these ideas and tips together with our recommendations to achieve success.

How Will you Fit Adventures into your Life?

To begin, you will need to decide how you are going to incorporate Adventures into your family's life. Depending on when you have available time, you could plan weekday or weekend Adventures. Weekend Adventures might make it easier to involve your spouse or the whole family. If you are at home during the weekdays, you could pair up with a friend, like we do, and explore during the day.

With whom will you go on your Adventures? Will it be your spouse, a friend, or just you and the kids? If you're going to find a friend to share your Adventures, you will need to decide who that will be. Look for someone with whom you get along well or someone you would like to know better and who has kids approximately the same ages as yours. You may want to try one or two Adventures before committing to a whole summer. If you want to plan weekly excursions, you'll need a partner who is willing to make this kind of commitment. That's not to say there can't be exceptions to a weekly schedule. We usually average about nine Adventures each summer, skipping a couple of weeks for vacations and camps.

As we shared in the last chapter, having an Adventure partner has many benefits. The Bible has some good advice for us in this area:

> You are better off to have a friend than to be all alone, because then you will get more enjoyment out of what you earn. If you fall, your friend can help you up. But if you fall without having a friend nearby, you are really in trouble.
>
> Ecclesiastes 4:9–10 (Contemporary English Version)

Neither of us has ever literally fallen down during an Adventure, but a partner can be there to help with many kinds of issues. A friend might help with reading a map, taking kids to the bathroom, or running to the car to fetch the first aid kit if someone scrapes a knee. We also share the joy of going through the experience together. A partner simply makes the time more enjoyable.

Can a group of friends plan Adventures? Sure they can. From time to time, another friend will join us on an Adventure. While this can be fun, it can also add complexity. With just two of us and our own children, we have more flexibility and can more easily come to agreement on last minute changes. For example, there have been many times we delayed an Adventure by an hour because the kids slept late. Other times we had planned on bringing lunches but changed our minds at the last minute because we didn't have anything convenient to pack. Additionally, if your group can all fit into a single vehicle, traveling can be more straightforward than with a caravan. We think that some of these smaller group benefits have been one of the reasons we've been successful.

Pick a Day

When are you going to have your Adventures? We almost always have our Adventure on Tuesdays. If you are doing weekend Adventures, maybe you will always plan them on the second Saturday of the month. It might sound restrictive to do it the same day every week or month, but it's really easier than having a varied schedule. We generally don't make any other commitments on Tuesdays. On occasion, we've come across attractions we want to see that are closed on Tuesdays and we will switch to a different day that week. We can be as flexible as we need to be, but it works well for both of us to have a standing date.

Plan your Adventures

The next step is to decide which outings have the most appeal and then design an itinerary. We have found that it works best to plan a schedule that is adjustable enough to allow for changes. During our first summer we didn't make our plans in advance. Each week we decided our next activity, sometimes as late as the night before. The next year, we sat down together in April and filled in our calendars. We found that it was much less stressful to decide everything in advance. We recommend making a schedule and sticking with it unless something arises that requires a change.

If you are planning summer Adventures, it's best to save any indoor Adventures for the end of the season. The temperature tends to get hotter towards the end of July and August and sometimes it's just too miserable to enjoy being outside. If we have an unusually hot or a rainy day early in the summer, we select something else from our plan that is indoors, with shelter and air conditioning, and move the outdoor excursion to a later date. This also helps minimize the time spent indoors when the weather is beautiful. This strategy provides the freedom to change plans while still keeping you on track to include all your planned Adventures for the summer.

If you are scheduling year round Adventures, plan your outdoor Adventures during the warmer months, but have a back-up activity in case the weather requires you to alter your plans.

Balance Activity Types

We have listed over 120 different attractions in this book. In the final section we have sorted the attractions into numerous categories such as museums, parks, animals, and historical sites. When we plan our summer, we try to select one or two destinations from each category. This broadens our experiences and keeps our outings refreshing for all of us. For example, one week we'll go to a botanical garden, the next week a factory tour, next a museum, and then a new park. Over the course of a summer you can learn some history, be entertained, get some exercise, reflect on art, and stimulate your minds in other ways. By scheduling a mix of Adventures, you'll find that if one week isn't a big hit, there will be something new and different to look forward to the next time. We also have a category for free attractions to help you meet your budget goals. An occasional splurge can be justified when we balance it with several free or low-cost outings.

Logistically Speaking

This book's data was accurate at the time of printing, but keep in mind that operating hours and admission fees can change. Be sure to check the operating schedules before visiting. Decide in advance who will drive and who will be in charge of directions or a map. Having a GPS unit certainly reduces the reliance on directions and maps. Not only does it route you to your destination, but it provides an estimated arrival time. A GPS or smartphone can also be used to find nearby restaurants and parks.

Don't Forget to Call

We have learned the principle "call ahead" the hard way. Websites are not always accurate, books may be out of date, and newspaper articles may have conflicting information. Once, we had heard about a restaurant where you eat ice cream while watching sky divers jump out of planes. They laughed when we called because this information had been out of date for ten years! We were relieved we didn't make that drive without checking our information first. A phone call is always your best option.

As another example, there was an historical village we had wanted to visit for years. According to their website, they were closed on our normal Adventure day, so we changed plans to visit on a different day. When we arrived, there were no guides working that day, all the buildings were locked, and it was raining. While we weren't charged to get in, we found ourselves walking through an historical village in the rain and looking at the outsides of buildings. If we had called ahead, we would have learned they were experiencing a temporary shortage of tour guides and could have made plans to visit another time.

Diffuse Disappointments

As hard as you work at making plans, sometimes Adventures don't turn out like you had hoped. But do not despair; they can still be redeemed! For instance, look for a nearby park and explore a playground. It's always prudent to pair any Adventure that might be risky, meaning the kids might not like it, with something you know they will enjoy. To continue the story of our rainy and disappointing visit to the historical village, afterwards we went to Build-A-Bear Workshop® at the mall and the kids had a great time. To avoid the need to improvise, you can be prepared for an alternate activity. When we planned our trip to Clifton Mill, an old-fashioned grist mill about an hour away, we weren't sure if the kids would enjoy the tour. In case this occurred, we also planned to dine at the adjoining restaurant that serves pancakes which we were positive the kids would love.

It is our recommendation to try some activities that you are uncertain the kids will enjoy. Sometimes our kids really surprise us by showing an interest in something that we wouldn't have anticipated. The Dayton Aviation Heritage National Historical Park has a small theater showing a documentary film about the Wright Brothers. We thought it might not appeal to young kids, but opted to see it anyway. Surprisingly, when the film ended, Terri's youngest daughter Camille, who was four at the time, declared that it was the best movie she'd ever seen and wanted to watch it again at home for movie night.

What's for Lunch?

If your Adventure will last more than half a day, you'll need to consider plans for lunch. We've tried several different options for lunches, but to save money we usually pack our own meal. One year we took turns packing lunches to give each other a break. However, sometimes it makes sense to eat in a restaurant as part of the Adventure. Our kids loved eating at Clifton Mill after taking a tour of the grist mill. Another restaurant Adventure is Sky Galley, where you can eat while watching planes take off and land at Lunken Airport. There are some weeks when we have so much going on that we give ourselves permission to eat out so that we can take one task off our to-do lists.

Turn an Adventure into an Education

If you are interested in carrying the theme of the Adventure through the week, you can supplement your outing with related books or activities.

Check out fiction and nonfiction books from the library that help you learn more about the subject. Or, watch a movie that enhances the experience. You could add other related activities, like crafts or games. We recommend starting with the Adventures, and adding other activities as time and energy permit, after you are in a comfortable routine.

Opportunities Abound

This book is filled with a diverse collection of recommended attractions to begin your Adventure planning. It includes all of our personal favorites compiled after our years of travels. We are constantly on the lookout for new ideas and encourage you to do the same. Remember to use local newspapers as a resource. In the summer and fall, they publish lists of U-pick farms for blueberries, strawberries, and apples. In addition, they itemize unique events, festivals, concerts, or plays around town. If you hear of something a friend has done, ask about it and write it down. If your kids like hiking, look into letterboxing (www.letterboxing.org) or geocaching (www.geocaching.com), which combine hiking with a mission of finding a hidden treasure. Be sure to look at the travel brochures while staying at a hotel. Stop at a visitor's center in your hometown or visit one in another city while traveling. Parks in your area or even a fast food or mall play area can also be great kid-pleasers. There are probably many entertaining destinations located near your neighborhood like bowling alleys, miniature golf, or go-carts. While these types of Adventures will almost always be a hit with your kids, try also to look beyond typical attractions. Especially when you are in another city, search for something unique to the area. Unique locations may end up being more memorable for your family than seeing the latest movie release. Keep your eyes and ears open and you are sure to find a memorable Adventure!

On your Mark, Get Set, Go!

In the following pages, you'll find many years' worth of our own Adventures. We wanted to be sure that all of our listings were "tested" by our kids, so at least one of our families has personally visited and approved all of them. Now, your next step is to follow our guidelines and start a new Adventure tradition with your kids. You will be encouraged by the excitement you see in your kids. Pick something you are sure your kids will like and create a new memory!

We know there are still more places to see and activities to do that aren't included in this edition. As we explore new places, we plan to post them on our Facebook page and tweet about them on Twitter. If you have a suggestion for a listing to include in a future edition of this book, please let us know, and we will be sure to check it out. We love hearing from people who have heard us speak and then planned their own Adventures. Please contact us and share your experiences. We wish you many priceless memories with your family as you start your own tradition of Adventures!

Email: contactus@adventuresaroundcincinnati.com
Website: www.adventuresaroundcincinnati.com
Facebook: Adventures Around Cincinnati
Twitter: AdventureCincy
Pinterest: AdventureCincy
Google+:   Adventures Around Cincinnati

Part Two

ATTRACTION LISTINGS

CENTRAL CINCINNATI
AND NORTHERN KENTUCKY

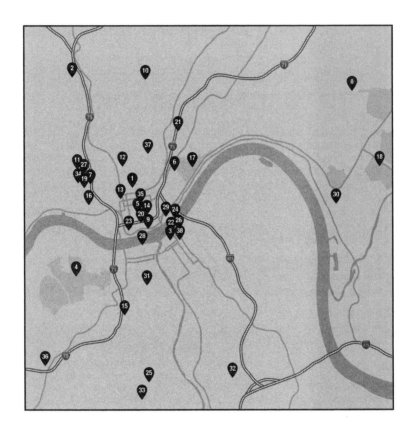

1 American Legacy Tours
2 American Sign Museum
3 BB Riverboats
4 Behringer-Crawford Museum
5 Carew Tower Observation Deck
6 Cincinnati Art Museum
7 Cincinnati History Museum at Cincinnati Museum Center
8 The Cincinnati Observatory
9 Cincinnati Reds Hall of Fame & Museum
10 Cincinnati Zoo & Botanical Garden
11 Duke Energy Children's Museum at Cincinnati Museum Center
12 Findlay Market
13 Fire Museum of Greater Cincinnati
14 Fountain Square
15 Garden of Hope
16 Greater Cincinnati Police Museum
17 Krohn Conservatory
18 Lunken Airport Playfield
19 Museum of Natural History and Science at Cincinnati Museum Center
20 National Underground Railroad Freedom Center
21 Neusole Glassworks
22 Newport Aquarium
23 Paul Brown Stadium Tour
24 Purple People Bridge
25 Railway Museum of Greater Cincinnati
26 Ride the Ducks - Newport
27 Robert D. Lindner Family OMNIMAX Theater at Cincinnati Museum Center
28 Roebling Murals
29 Sawyer Point Park & Yeatman's Cove
30 Sky Galley Restaurant at Lunken Airport
31 St. Mary's Cathedral Basilica of the Assumption
32 Sunrock Farm
33 Totter's Otterville
34 Tower A at Cincinnati Union Terminal
35 UnMuseum at the Contemporary Arts Center
36 Vent Haven Museum
37 William Howard Taft National Historic Site
38 World Peace Bell

AMERICAN LEGACY TOURS

Address: 1332 Vine Street, Cincinnati, OH 45202

Phone: (859) 951-8560

Website: www.americanlegacytours.com

Hours: Check website for tour departure times
            Tours are generally scheduled on weekends

Cost: $15–30 per person

Ages: 10 and up

Stroller and wheelchair friendly: No. Strollers or wheelchairs may be used on the street, but the tour contains many steps to navigate.

Length of visit: Tours last from 90 minutes to 2 ½ hours
Allow time to park before your tour begins

Description and comments:
    American Legacy Tours has been providing tours in Cincinnati since 2010. They specialize in walking tours of the city from an historical perspective. The tours generally begin in the Over-The-Rhine neighborhood (also known as the Gateway District). Each tour takes you into historic buildings including churches, saloons, and theaters. The knowledgeable tour guides share stories about the history of the OTR area; the role of the German settlers in the area; the history of religion, industry, and politics in the region; and many other interesting historical facts. The guides will surprise you with anecdotes of famous (and sometimes infamous) people who lived in or passed through the area along with details of the interesting history of how these buildings were used.

The website contains a full listing of tours available. Some of the tours currently offered are the Queen City Underground Tour, the Newport Gangster Tour, the Civil War Tour, Rookwood Factory and Market Tour, and the Queen City is Haunted Walking Tour. During the Christmas season, they also offer the Spirit of Christmas Tour, which includes stops in several churches, a living nativity, and historic tales of Christmas traditions which originated in Cincinnati.

Their Queen City Underground Tour is one of the top five Underground Tours in the U.S. as rated by *National Geographic* magazine. This tour visits historical buildings and churches while also descending under the city into recently discovered tunnels that were used by the Cincinnati brewing industry.

These tours require walking for several blocks, so take that into consideration if bringing younger children. You know your children best and know if they will be interested in the historical content of the tours and if they are capable of walking the whole tour. The Newport Gangster Tour contains some mature content regarding the illegal activity that was once so prevalent in the area. We would recommend that it is a tour best suited for adults.

AMERICAN SIGN MUSEUM

<u>Address:</u>   1330 Monmouth Street, Cincinnati, OH 45225

<u>Phone:</u>   (513) 541-6366

<u>Website:</u>   www.signmuseum.org

<u>Hours:</u>   Wednesday–Saturday: 10 a.m.–4 p.m.
Guided tours at 11 a.m. and 2 p.m.
Sunday: Noon–4 p.m.
Guided tour at 2 p.m.
Schedule guided tours in advance to ensure availability; can be done online

<u>Cost:</u> $15 Adults
Free Children under 12
$10 Seniors

<u>Ages:</u>   4 and up

<u>Stroller and wheelchair friendly:</u> Yes

<u>Length of visit:</u> 1–2 hours

<u>Description and comments:</u>

Most people see signs every day and don't think much about them. After a visit to the American Sign Museum, you won't look at signs the same way again. The American Sign Museum has been around for several years, but moved to a new location in the Camp Washington neighborhood in 2012. You can either tour the museum yourself or take a guided tour. We recommend the guided tour; you will get much more out of your visit that way.

The tour starts with a brief history of the types of letters used in signs, starting with wooden letters. Visitors learn the evolution of sign-making materials from wood to metal to glass to plastic. See how electric signs have changed over the years. Brightly lit neon signs lend a festive atmosphere to the museum. Kids recognize the Big Boy® figure from Frisch's and learn how the figure has changed over the years, going from striped to checkered pants and changes to the slingshot in his back pocket. You'll also see several examples of trade signs that need no writing at all because the shape of the sign tells potential customers exactly what kind of establishment it is.

The museum's collection is comprised of signs from 1890 to 1972. One of the highlights of a visit is the Main Street exhibit that simulates a street in the center of a small town. Storefronts were created with amazing attention to detail and additional signs are displayed in the windows. Each section represents a different era and the overall effect is impressive.

Another favorite feature is the sign shop located on the premises. Neonworks of Cincinnati is located in the building and weekday museum visitors can watch them work. Our kids were fascinated as they watched the skilled craftsmen heat and bend glass. Please note that Neonworks typically operates on weekdays only.

This is an excellent museum for generations of families to visit together. Many of the signs might spark conversations about how times were different when the grandparents were growing up.

BB RIVERBOATS

Address: 101 Riverboat Row, Newport, KY 41071

Phone: (859) 261-8500
(800) 261-8586

Website: www.bbriverboats.com

Hours: Daily sightseeing cruises, Memorial Day through Labor Day

90-minute sightseeing cruises; see website for departure times.

Boarding time is 20 minutes prior to cruise time.

Dining, holiday and special cruises also available; check website for details.

Cost: $20–22 Adults
$14–16 Children (4–12)
Free Children 3 and under, but ticket required

Check for discounts in the Entertainment Book.

Ages: All ages

Stroller and wheelchair friendly: Yes

Length of visit: 2 hours (allow extra time for boarding)

Description and comments:

Enjoy a view of Cincinnati and Northern Kentucky's landmarks from the river. Go up to the open air top deck for the best views or sit in air-conditioned comfort on a lower deck. The captain broadcasts a commentary during the 90-minute cruise, pointing out landmarks and sharing some history. Older children may take an interest in the commentary, but it's best to bring some toys or coloring books to occupy younger children if they start to get restless. Since riverboats are an important part of Cincinnati's history, we think everyone should take a riverboat cruise at least once. A snack bar and restrooms are available. Each child receives a free ice cream sandwich on either the Harbor Cruise or the Ice Cream Social Cruise.

If you have preschool age children, consider booking one of the specialty cruises for kids. During the "Pirates of the Ohio" cruise, little pirates receive a pirate hat, eye patch, and treasure map, and play pirate games. Little girls can gussy up for the "Princess Cruise" where they will receive royal treatment. Aspiring super heroes get official Super Hero Training aboard the "Super Hero Cruise."

BEHRINGER-CRAWFORD MUSEUM

Address: 1600 Montague Road, Covington, KY 41011

Phone: (859) 491-4003

Website: www.bcmuseum.org

Hours: Tuesday–Saturday: 10 a.m.–5 p.m.
            Sunday: 1–5 p.m.
            Closed Mondays and all national holidays

Cost: $7 Adults
            $4 Children (3–17)
            $6 Seniors (60+)

Ages: 2 and up

Stroller and wheelchair friendly: Yes

Length of visit: 1–3 hours

Description and comments:

Located in Devou Park, this museum celebrates the heritage of Northern Kentucky. Kids explore hands-on exhibits while learning about Kentucky's natural and cultural history. Upon entering, you can't miss the *Kentucky* streetcar, the last streetcar to run in Northern Kentucky. Visitors are not permitted to board the streetcar, but there are several passengers aboard and you can push buttons to hear their stories. There is an introductory film that is helpful to watch. Most of the film is narrated by a couple of young teens and there are computer-generated graphics, making it appealing to kids. One thing that we love about this museum is that nearly every room has a play area for young kids to keep them occupied while parents and older siblings view the exhibits. These include train tables, doll houses, and kitchen toys.

Each of the four levels has one or more themes. The first floor focuses on rails. One of our favorite exhibits is the model train display. There are nearly a dozen buttons that activate trains, trolleys, lights, and sounds. The best feature is a tunnel that goes underneath the display with bubble windows on the inside of the model so that kids (and adventurous adults) can view it from the inside. The theme of the second floor is roads. You sit in a 1959 Buick Electra convertible and watch a film at the drive-in about lifestyles of the 1950's.

The third floor is the largest floor and contains exhibits on industry, rivers, immigrants, and tourism. There is also a section for rotating exhibits. Make sure you find the famous two-headed calf and shrunken head. Kids love the Roebling Suspension Bridge and interactive packet boat exhibit that has a dress-up area. The fourth floor includes the upper deck of the packet boat, a display on airport runways, and a stuffed bear.

CAREW TOWER OBSERVATION DECK

<u>Address:</u>   441 Vine Street, Cincinnati, OH 45202
              Corner of Fifth and Vine across from
              Fountain Square

<u>Phone:</u>   (513) 579-9735 Observation Deck
              (513) 241-3888 to arrange for group discounts

<u>Hours:</u>   Monday–Friday: 10 a.m.–6 p.m.
              Saturday and Sunday: 10 a.m.–7 p.m.

<u>Cost:</u> $2 Adults
              $1 Children (6–11)
              Free Children 5 and under
              Call ahead for group discounts

<u>Ages:</u>   All ages

<u>Stroller and wheelchair friendly:</u> No

<u>Length of visit:</u> 1 hour

<u>Description and comments:</u>

For many years, Carew Tower was the tallest building in Cincinnati. Now it is the second tallest. It rises 49 stories and 574 feet over downtown Cincinnati near the Ohio River. To visit the observation deck, ride the elevator to the 45th floor. At this point, you'll need to leave your stroller behind. Next, board a tiny elevator and ride to the 48th floor, then climb the steel stairway to your destination. On a clear day, visitors can see for miles into Ohio, Kentucky, and Indiana. The observation deck is appropriate for all ages, but be aware that smaller kids will need a boost to see over the wall. This can be challenging if you have several kids who all need to be held in order to see the view. The wall is approximately 42" tall. Kids taller than about 54" will be able to see easily over the fence without help. The wind is sometimes strong, so be prepared with a jacket or sweater. Be aware that there are no public restrooms in Carew Tower. The closest facilities are across the street at Fountain Square.

Carew Tower is a must-see attraction in Cincinnati. The building itself is a National Historic Landmark, and the view is spectacular. While visiting, notice the Art Deco design of the building. One interesting fact is that construction began on Carew Tower in September 1929, one month before the stock market crashed. The work continued, but only the first three floors were built with the impressive details. After this, plain brick was used on the remaining floors.

Parking is available in the Carew Tower or Fountain Square parking garages. Street parking is also available.

CINCINNATI ART MUSEUM

Address: 953 Eden Park Drive, Cincinnati, OH 45202

Phone: (513) 639-2995 General
            (513) 639-2971 Education Center
            (877) 472-4226

Website: www.cincinnatiartmuseum.org

Hours: Tuesday–Sunday: 11 a.m.–5 p.m.
            Closed some holidays

Cost: Museum admission is free
            $4 Parking

Ages: 8 and up

Stroller and wheelchair friendly: Yes

Length of visit: 1–4 hours

Description and comments:

Your first stop at the Cincinnati Art Museum should be the front desk where you can pick up a Family Guide and map. The Family Guide, which changes monthly, often includes a scavenger hunt. This gives the kids a mission as they explore the galleries. Upon completion of the scavenger hunt, return it to the front desk to receive a prize. Another way we have found to keep the kids' interest is to ask them to pick out their favorite piece in each gallery and tell us why they like it.

Most of the museum is decidedly hands-off (they might scold kids even for standing too close to the art), but there are a few places that have hands-on exhibits, including galleries 137 and 141 in the Asian art section. The museum has paintings from well-known artists such as Picasso,

Van Gogh, Monet, Manet, Pissarro, Renoir, and Cézanne. It also has other forms of art such as sculpture, pottery, woodcarving, and metalwork, and includes art from many time periods and parts of the world. If you choose to take younger children into the galleries, we recommend keeping them in a stroller.

The Cincinnati Art Museum has many programs for children and families. Some programs are free and some require a fee. These run from September through May. Free programs include Family ARTventures (Saturdays at 1 p.m. and Sundays at 3 p.m.), Family First Saturday (first Saturday of the month, 1–4 p.m.), and Wee Wednesdays (last Wednesday of the month, 10–11:30 a.m.). Check the website for information on other programs.

CINCINNATI HISTORY MUSEUM AT CINCINNATI MUSEUM CENTER

Address: 1301 Western Avenue, Cincinnati, OH 45203

Phone: (513) 287-7000

Website: www.cincymuseum.org

Hours: Monday–Saturday: 10 a.m.–5 p.m.
            Sunday: 11 a.m.–6 p.m.

Cost: $8.50 Adults
            $6.50 Children (3–12)
            $4.50 Children (1–2)
            Free Children under 1 with adult
            $7.50 Seniors (60+)

            $6 Parking

            Discounts are offered if you visit more than one
            museum or see an OMNIMAX film. Check
            website for more information. Check for
            discounts in the Entertainment Book.

            An annual family membership to all three
            museums (Duke Energy Children's Museum,
            Museum of Natural History and Science, and
            Cincinnati History Museum) with free parking
            and free or discounted admission to 200+
            museums worldwide is $130. We highly
            recommend this option.

Ages: 3 and up

Stroller and wheelchair friendly: Yes

Length of visit: 2–4 hours

Description and comments:

The Cincinnati History Museum opens a window into Cincinnati's past. Upon entering the museum, you find yourself immersed in a model of Cincinnati with each neighborhood set in a different decade. The model includes working trains, inclines, and moving vehicles. Learn about the history of each neighborhood at interactive computer stations. Each month the museum creates an "I Spy" challenge for kids in which they must locate objects that have been hidden in the model. Check at the information desk to find out the challenge of the month. Behind the model, there are train tables to keep the little ones occupied. The trains must be checked out at the information desk. There is no charge, but they will keep your ID until you return the trains.

Next you pass through the Cincinnati Goes to War exhibit, where you climb aboard a streetcar and listen to a commentary. Wander past other displays and push the buttons to hear stories about people's lives during that time. Continuing through the museum, you find exhibits on Cincinnati's settlers, including Native Americans, pioneers, and immigrants. Watch an interactive video on the earthworks built by Native Americans. Visit a log cabin where there are often demonstrations such as carding wool or sewing. Kids learn about Ohio's transportation history by maneuvering a canal boat through a canal with locks at a wooden model built especially for kids. Then climb aboard a model of a flatboat, the moving van of the frontier. Learn about how pioneers built these boats, then disassembled them at their destination and used the wood to build their houses. Kids try this themselves at a kid-sized version of a boat and house with removable boards.

On the lower level, you'll feel like you've stepped into another time at Cincinnati's Public Landing. Step aboard a recreated steamboat and learn what makes the paddle wheel turn. Visit a working print shop and see how documents were printed before computers were invented. Peek in the windows of various shops and interact with costumed interpreters. Finally, visit the recreated 1910 machine shop with working machinery.

Frequent Museum Center visitors should look into "employment" for kids ages 6 and up at the C.U.T. (Cincinnati Union Terminal) House Detective Agency. When new detectives are "hired," they will be issued a case file, notebook, and pencil, and are sent out to solve mysteries. They must visit different parts of the museum to solve the mysteries and then report back to the Chief Inspector with their findings. They earn money (in special C.U.T. currency) for each mystery they solve and can spend it on merchandise in the detective store. Detectives are recognized with promotions to higher ranks in the organization as they solve more mysteries. There is a one-time fee of $5 to participate in this fun program. Check the Calendar of Events on the website to find out about the many free scheduled activities in the museum.

THE CINCINNATI OBSERVATORY

Address: 3489 Observatory Place, Cincinnati, OH 45208

Phone: (513) 321-5186

Website: www.cincinnatiobservatory.org

Hours: Check website for program schedule

Cost: $5–10 per person
            Varies by program

Ages: 6 and up

Stroller and wheelchair friendly: First floor only

Length of visit: 1–2 hours

Description and comments:

The Cincinnati Observatory in Mount Lookout is a National Historic Landmark that is a fully functioning 19th century observatory. The Herget Building was built in 1873 and was designed by architect Samuel Hannaford who also designed many other Cincinnati landmarks including City Hall and Music Hall. The smaller Mitchel Building is home to the oldest telescope in the United States.

An ideal first Adventure to The Cincinnati Observatory is to attend their Astronomy Nights program.   First, visitors hear an informative presentation about astronomy lasting about 30 minutes. Following the talk, take part in a guided stargaze as you view the skies through one of their telescopes. Kids are thrilled to see planets and learn how to identify constellations. This public program is held on most Thursday and Friday nights and requires an advance reservation. Make reservations online or by phone at least a week in advance because this program does fill up. It is recommended for ages 7 and up and admission is a suggested $5 on Thursdays. On Fridays, the cost is $7 for adults and $5 for children under 18.

The observatory holds free public stargazes twice monthly on Saturday nights if skies are clear. These gazes are held at Stonelick Lake State Park, east of Milford, where the sky is darker than in the city and suburbs. Bring your own telescope or look through one of the large telescopes set up by either the astronomers from the observatory or a friendly amateur astronomer. For dates and directions to these star parties, see www.cincinnatiobservatory.org/stonelick-lake.html.

Cincinnati Observatory Astronomer Dean Regas is one of the co-hosts of the popular PBS television program *Star Gazers*. This program is an excellent resource to learn more about the night sky. View current episodes on the observatory's website or at www.stargazersonline.org.

Historical Tours of The Cincinnati Observatory are held on the second and fourth Sunday of each month from 1–4 p.m. These tours showcase the architecture and history of the observatory. Tours generally start on the hour and last about an hour. The cost is $5 per person.

CINCINNATI REDS HALL OF FAME & MUSEUM

Address: 100 Joe Nuxhall Way, Cincinnati, OH 45202

Phone: (513) 765-7923

Website: www.redsmuseum.org

Hours: November–March
Tuesday–Sunday: 10 a.m.–5 p.m.

April–October (Non-game days)
Saturday and Sunday: 10 a.m.–5 p.m.

April–October (Game Days)
Afternoon Games: 10 a.m.–two hours after end
of game
Evening Games: 10 a.m.–8 p.m.

Cost: $10 Adults
$8 Children (5–17)
Free Children 4 and under, active military,
and veterans
$8 Seniors (60+)

Ages: 3 and up

Stroller and wheelchair friendly: Yes

Length of visit: 2 hours

Description and comments:

If you have a baseball fan in your family, be sure to visit the Cincinnati Reds Hall of Fame & Museum. Here you learn the history of the Reds from 1869 to the present day, and about the Hall of Famers. Start your visit by sitting in the grandstand and watching a 10-minute retrospective on the history of the Reds. You'll see a number of displays including a view of the exact spot Pete Rose's record-breaking 4,192nd hit landed and a rose garden with a white rose bush commemorating the exact location of this hit.

Visit the Reds Front Office where you'll discover the history behind famous trades. The traditional gallery contains oodles of baseball memorabilia. In the Play Ball Gallery, try your hand at fielding, batting, and pitching. Feel a 95-mph fast ball zoom past you, stand on the mound and attempt pitching a ball into the strike zone, then leap into the air to snag that important catch. Kids under six have their own play space including small lockers complete with a dress up area containing Reds jerseys.

Pick up the microphone and jump into a broadcast by Marty Brennaman and Joe Nuxhall and call a close play for them. Next, listen to Marty and Joe call the same play. Relax on the "front porch" and listen to Waite Hoyt and Joe Nuxhall recall memories from their careers.

The Ultimate Reds Room is decorated like a home rec room including a vast collection of bobbleheads, pennants, signs, and baseball cards. Watch a show with bloopers and highlights while sitting in seats from Riverfront stadium.

Relive the glory days of the Big Red Machine and walk among figures of famous players. Scores of items are dedicated to explaining the history of baseball through the years, including the World Series trophies. Finally, enter the Hall of Fame, where each Hall of Famer is commemorated with a plaque.

The Hall of Fame conducts tours of Great American Ball Park, the Home of the Reds. Call for tour schedules and pricing.

CINCINNATI ZOO & BOTANICAL GARDEN

Address: 3400 Vine Street, Cincinnati, OH 45220

Phone: (513) 281-4700

Website: www.cincyzoo.org

Hours: Daily
January–May: 9 a.m.–5 p.m.
May–September: 9 a.m.–6 p.m.
September–December: 9 a.m.–5 p.m.

Cost: $15 Adults
$10 Children (2–12)
$10 Seniors (62+)
$8 Parking

Additional fees for rides and 4D theater. Package pricing available. Check for discounts with AAA, Kroger card, or Entertainment Book.

Ages: All ages

Stroller and wheelchair friendly: Yes

Length of visit: 2–6 hours

Description and comments:

What can we say? Cincinnati has a great zoo! The Zagat Survey calls it the number one attraction in Cincinnati and one of the top zoos in the nation. Before you go, check the website for self-guided tours with attractions specially suited for kids or for ideas for a rainy or cold day.

You'll find many exhibits at the zoo for everyone to explore. It's amusing to visit Gibbon Island to watch these animals swinging and chasing each other on their natural playground. Stop by Giraffe Ridge and feed the giraffes crackers from the palm of your hand. Gorillas, manatees, polar bears, penguins, insects, eagles, and wolves are other favorite attractions. Visit Siegfried & Roy's famous white lions. Don't miss the petting area in the Children's Zoo, either.

Many inside attractions make the zoo fun for a cold or rainy day, too. Manatee Springs, 4D Special FX Theatre, Nocturnal House and the Discovery Forest are just a few of the inside attractions that will keep you from being soaked if the weather turns bad.

Also, gaze at the stunning annuals, perennials, trees, plants and grasses that make up the Botanical Gardens. See the zoo website for more information on the different varieties of plants.

Train rides are available (for an extra fee), along with a carousel ride.

DUKE ENERGY CHILDREN'S MUSEUM AT CINCINNATI MUSEUM CENTER

Address: 1301 Western Avenue, Cincinnati, OH 45203

Phone: (513) 287-7000
(800) 733-2077

Website: www.cincymuseum.org

Hours: Monday–Saturday: 10 a.m.–5 p.m.
Sunday: 11 a.m.–6 p.m.

Cost: $8.50 Adults
$6.50 Children (3–12)
$4.50 Children (1–2)
Free Children under 1 with adult
$7.50 Seniors (60+)

$6 Parking

Discounts are offered if you visit more than one museum or see an OMNIMAX film. Check website for more information. Check for discounts in the Entertainment Book.

An annual family membership to all three museums (Duke Energy Children's Museum, Museum of Natural History and Science, and Cincinnati History Museum) with free parking and free or discounted admission to 200+ museums worldwide is $130. We highly recommend this option.

Ages: 1–12

Stroller and wheelchair friendly: Yes

<u>Length of visit:</u> 2–5 hours

<u>Description and comments:</u>

The Duke Energy Children's Museum is one of three museums in the Cincinnati Museum Center complex at Union Terminal. It has consistently ranked in the top ten children's museums in the world. Little Sprouts Farm is a separate area for families with children age four and under. It includes an area with slides, play gardens, a sand table, a pretend row boat, story times, and puppet shows. It also contains a Parent Resource Area and a private area for nursing moms and babies. The entrance to Little Sprouts Farm is supervised to prevent little ones from leaving without you. Park your stroller in the "parking lot" outside the farm and prepare to spend hours with your preschoolers.

Kids (ages 3–7) pretend to be grown-ups in Kids Town, an area including a grocery store, diner, veterinary office, kitchen, and play house. Buying groceries, delivering mail, taking animal x-rays, and ordering and preparing meals to serve to customers at the diner are some of the activities for this age group.

In Energy Zone, the giant ball play area, the kids grab a bag and scurry to collect thousands of balls off of the floor. Use the blasting air jets to float a ball in midair. Try to pedal an exercise bike to power a ball conveyor, launch a ball into a basket using air pressure, and be prepared for a giant shower of colorful balls when you hear the alarm bell ring.

Find three stories of climbing fun in The Woods. Your children will be thrilled to climb in the trees, whiz down the slide, cross rope bridges, search for fossils, and explore a small cave. The Woods houses a large aquarium filled with fish and turtles. Your children can search for the secret tunnel ending "inside" the water. This area is best for kids over age five who can navigate the sometimes challenging climbing areas.

You will want to visit the many other areas in the museum where you can try to assemble a large arch with foam shapes, construct a skyscraper using blocks, pound nails into buildings, visit children who live in other countries, splash in the water play area, load "rocks" into a crane, and dump them into a dump truck. Watch for special posted activities your children might enjoy, too.

The entrance to Union Terminal contains a Rotunda with a few lunch options. An abundance of tables are available, and you are permitted to carry in your lunch. While in the Rotunda, be sure to look at the ceiling to observe the two 20' x 105' mosaics depicting the history of Cincinnati. These mosaics were commissioned in 1932. Other mosaics are found near the entrance to the OMNIMAX Theatre. The Museum Center originally had many more of these murals decorating the building. During renovations, these murals have been moved to the Greater Cincinnati/Northern Kentucky International Airport.

The Children's Museum can be crowded in the mornings, with fewer visitors after lunch. If your children have outgrown naps, afternoon is your best bet. Remember to bring a change of clothes in case your kids get carried away in the water play area. You won't want to leave this fun-filled museum!

FINDLAY MARKET

Address: 1801 Race Street, Cincinnati, OH 45202

Phone: (513) 665-4839

Website: www.findlaymarket.org

Hours: Findlay Market is open year round
            Tuesday–Friday: 9 a.m.–6 p.m.
            Saturday: 8 a.m.–6 p.m.
            Sunday: 10 a.m.–4 p.m.

            The Farmers Market is open seasonally
            Saturday: 8 a.m.–2 p.m.
            Sunday: 10 a.m.–2 p.m.
            Thursday: 3 p.m.–6 p.m.

Cost: Free admission
            Pay for parking in the Findlay Market lot

Ages: All ages

Stroller and wheelchair friendly: Yes

Length of visit: 2–3 hours

Description and comments:

   If you're looking for an Adventure where you can shop,
eat, and explore a location on the National Register of
Historic Places, then Findlay Market is the place for you.
Findlay Market has been in operation as a local shopping
and gathering spot since 1855. The market contains an
extensive variety of products to purchase including local
produce, tempting baked goods, diverse ethnic offerings,
teas, coffees, olive oils, ice cream, natural products, crafts,
and furniture. They also offer a wide selection of fresh
meats, sausages, and seafood. The market is divided into

an indoor Market House, many open air vendors, outside store fronts, and an outdoor Farmer's Market.

Findlay Market also has plenty of choices of restaurants sure to satisfy every taste. The restaurants range from outdoor grills serving up burgers to a variety of ethnic restaurants to a Beer Garden (open only on the weekends). The Beer Garden serves local beers and showcases live music on Sundays.

This is an Adventure suitable for all ages. Even kids who aren't normally shoppers will find interesting items to look at, taste, and take home. If you have kids who need a mission, you might ask them to search for the biggest fish, the most exotic spice, or the most unique vegetable they can find. They might spot a giant cookie, a delicious strawberry covered waffle, or a refreshing scoop of ice cream on their visit.

You might want to pack a cooler in your car in order to transport your fresh meats or fish home with you. Many of the vendors accept only cash, so be sure to stop at the ATM before you arrive. Make a shopping list before you go or just browse and see what tempts you while you shop. Findlay Market is a Cincinnati tradition that is sure to bring a smile to your face!

FIRE MUSEUM OF GREATER CINCINNATI

Address: 315 W. Court Street, Cincinnati, OH 45202

Phone: (513) 621-5553

Website: www.cincyfiremuseum.com

Hours: Tuesday–Saturday: 10 a.m.–4 p.m.
           Closed holidays

Cost: $8 Adults
           $6 Children (7–17)
           Free Children 6 and under, with adult or
           senior admission
           $6 Seniors (65+)

           Parking is in metered spots on street. Bring
           coins to feed meter.

Ages: 2 and up

Stroller and wheelchair friendly: Yes

Length of visit: 1–2 hours

Description and comments:

   A trip to the Cincinnati Fire Museum is both
educational and entertaining. A favorite for young kids
is the cab of a fire engine. Kids can climb into it, push
buttons to turn on the lights, and pretend they are off
to fight a fire. Everyone can slide down a fire pole to
the lower level and watch a movie about fire safety. The
history of firefighting in Cincinnati is explained starting
from its earliest days with a bucket brigade. Kids like to
pretend to pump water with an old style hand pumper. A
safe house exhibit teaches about fire safety in the home.
Try out the interactive computer exhibits. Older kids may

show an interest in the exhibits on antique fire engines and equipment.

FOUNTAIN SQUARE

Address: 520 Vine Street, Cincinnati, OH 45202

Phone: (513) 979-4738

Website: www.myfountainsquare.com

Hours: Always open
           Call for skating hours

Cost: Free to visit Fountain Square
           $3 Admission for skating
           $3 Skate rental

Ages: All ages

Stroller and wheelchair friendly: Yes

Length of visit: 30 minutes–2 hours

Description and comments:

Fountain Square is at the heart of downtown Cincinnati and features garden-like landscaping, tables with umbrellas and chairs, a full-color 30.5' x 42.5' LED video board, and the centerpiece fountain, *The Genius of Water*. Uniformed Ambassadors are always present to keep Fountain Square clean and safe.

Tyler Davidson Fountain is the focal point of Fountain Square. It was dedicated in 1871. The nine-foot-tall *Genius of Water* stands in the center of the fountain with other figures surrounding it showing the practical and recreational uses of water. Walk the perimeter of the fountain and notice the different animals and people on each side. The Water Wall is the other amusing feature at Fountain Square. A sheet of water pours down the wall and also spouts up from the ground. Kids might get a little wet running through and putting their hands in the water.

Fountain Square offers seasonal entertainment. Summertime brings concerts, movies, and more. In the winter, Fountain Square offers a public ice skating rink. Bring your own skates or rent them there for some cold-weather outdoor fun. Check the website for the activity and event calendar.

Surrounding Fountain Square are many shops and restaurants, including Graeter's famous ice cream. It is also fun to watch the horse drawn carriages circling the square.

Parking is available in the Fountain Square Garage. Enter the garage from Vine Street or Walnut Street for convenient access to Fountain Square.

GARDEN OF HOPE

<u>Address:</u>   699 Edgecliff Street, Covington, KY 41014

<u>Phone:</u>   (859) 491-1777

<u>Hours:</u>   Tours by appointment only
            Grounds are open daylight hours
            Good Friday: Open for tours, call for hours
            Easter Sunrise Service: 7 a.m.

<u>Cost:</u>   Donations appreciated

<u>Ages:</u>   All ages

<u>Stroller and wheelchair friendly:</u> Stroller friendly,
but not wheelchair accessible

<u>Length of visit:</u> 1–2 hours

<u>Description and comments:</u>

The Garden of Hope is a 2.5-acre garden containing an exact replica of Jesus' tomb. An architect in Jerusalem was hired to take the exact measurements so the tomb could be replicated here. The grounds contain a small, Spanish-style chapel and a carpenter's shop like the one Joseph would have worked in. The carpenter's shop includes historic tools donated by Israeli Prime Minister David Ben Gurion in 1956. The shop houses a mural depicting life in a Palestinian carpenter shop. One of the paving stones at the chapel is an actual stone from the location where Jesus preached the Sermon on the Mount. The garden includes an Italian marble statue of Jesus and authentic stones from the Good Samaritan Inn, the Jordan River, and Solomon's Temple. The grounds are landscaped with over 500 rocks, trees, and plants from Jerusalem.

Very few people in the area know about this gem of a park. Pastor Ed Kirkwood and tour guide Steve Cummins would love to have more people visit and show off the garden. The tour is interesting and you'll hear some history and explanations of the park and browse the insides of all the buildings. The view of Covington and downtown Cincinnati is spectacular from the garden. The Garden is open during the Labor Day Weekend Fireworks with hamburgers, hotdogs, live music, and a view of the fireworks away from the crowds. Bring a dish to share, a donation, and some folding chairs.

GREATER CINCINNATI POLICE MUSEUM

Address: Currently relocating; check website for new
            address

Phone: (513) 300-3664

Website: www.gcphs.com

Hours: Tuesday, Thursday, and Saturday:
            10 a.m.–4 p.m.

Cost: Free, Donations Accepted

Ages: 8 and up

Stroller and wheelchair friendly: Yes

Length of visit: 1–2 hours

Description and comments:

The Greater Cincinnati Police Museum is filled with historic artifacts, stories, and memorabilia covering over 200 years of history about the police force. Some of the collections include the history and development of police uniforms, a display of murder weapons, the evolution of police weapons, and an interactive switchboard and dispatch station. They have walkie-talkies that are a hit with the kids as they pretend to battle crime. One of the more surprising displays is the loyal police dog, Handsome, who, at his passing, was preserved and is on display at the museum. You will find badge collections, a Memorial Wall dedicated to officers who have given their lives in the line of duty, historical photographs, and many other displays helping visitors understand this history of law enforcement.

Museum docents include active or retired police officers who guide you through the museum explaining the exhibits and sharing personal stories with you. If you prefer a self-guided tour, you are also welcome to explore the museum at your own pace. Young detectives visiting the tour receive plastic badges and a detective notebook to complete as they hear clues given by the docents. Group tours of the museum are also offered. On these tours, docents explain how science, math, and chemistry all play a role in forensics and emphasize that studying hard helps lead to success in life.

A visit to this museum makes a nice addition to other downtown Adventures such as Carew Tower, Fountain Square, or one of the many downtown parks like Sawyer Point or Smale Riverfront Park.

At the time of publication, The Greater Cincinnati Police Museum is relocating to a new building. Their website will have current information on location and opening date.

KROHN CONSERVATORY

Address: 1501 Eden Park Drive, Cincinnati, OH 45202

Phone: (513) 421-4086

Website: www.cincinnatiparks.com/krohn

Hours: Tuesday–Sunday: 10 a.m.–5 p.m.
            Open Mondays during Butterfly and Holiday
            Shows only

Cost: Butterfly and Holiday Shows:
            $7 Adults
            $4 Children (5–12)
            Free Children 4 and under

            All other times:
            $3 Adults
            $2 Children (5–12)
            Free Children 4 and under

Ages: All ages

Stroller and wheelchair friendly: Yes

Length of visit: 1–2 hours

Description and comments:

Located in Eden Park, Krohn Conservatory houses more than 3,500 plant species from all over the world. Walk into the Palm House and feel as though you have been transported into a rainforest, surrounded by palm trees and other tropical plants, and a waterfall. Next, visit the Desert House with its cacti and other succulents. The conservatory also has collections of bonsai, orchids, and a tropical house. One room is reserved for seasonal displays and events. Our favorite is the Butterfly Show, held each year from mid-April to mid-June. Bright flowers fill the room and butterflies flutter around, landing on flowers and sometimes on people. Kids will be delighted trying to hold one on their finger. Stop by the craft room where kids can make a simple craft. It is best to attend on a sunny day, when butterflies are the most active.

The Holiday Floral Show is another favorite for families. It features a miniature railway and Cincinnati landmarks, poinsettias, and other botanical delights.

LUNKEN AIRPORT PLAYFIELD

<u>Address:</u>   4740 Playfield Lane, Cincinnati, OH 45226

<u>Phone:</u>   (513) 321-7333

<u>Website:</u>   www.cincyrec.org/search/facility.aspx?id=408

<u>Hours:</u>   Land of Make Believe:
Hours are seasonal and weather-dependent; generally open 10 a.m.–6 p.m. during the summer and Noon–4 p.m. in spring and fall.

Playground is free during off hours; use back gate for entrance. Restrooms not accessible during off hours.

<u>Cost:</u> $1 Children 12 and under (for the Land of Make Believe)
Free Adults

<u>Ages:</u>   1–9

<u>Stroller and wheelchair friendly:</u> Yes

<u>Length of visit:</u> 2–3 hours

<u>Description and comments:</u>

There are two playgrounds here to encourage kids to burn off some energy. The Land of Make Believe is fenced in so your little ones can't escape when you're not looking. Parents will be grateful for the shade that this park provides. It contains three large climbing structures and many other features including a sandbox to satisfy the younger kids. The $1 fee is truly worth it. The other playground is called the Spirit of '76 and is sunnier and not fenced in. There is no fee to play at this playground. You will find indoor air-conditioned bathrooms and a snack bar. The area also includes a golf course (regular and par 3), walking trails, tennis courts, and a baseball field. For lunch, either use the many picnic tables in the park or dine at the nearby Sky Galley restaurant (see separate listing).

MUSEUM OF NATURAL HISTORY AND SCIENCE AT CINCINNATI MUSEUM CENTER

Address: 1301 Western Avenue, Cincinnati, OH 45203

Phone: (513) 287-7000

Website: www.cincymuseum.org

Hours: Monday–Saturday: 10 a.m.–5 p.m.
Sunday: 11 a.m.–6 p.m.

Cost: $8.50 Adults
$6.50 Children (3–12)
$4.50 Children (1–2)
Free Children under 1 with adult
$7.50 Seniors (60+)

$6 Parking

Discounts are offered if you visit more than one museum or see an OMNIMAX film. Check website for more information. Check for discounts in the Entertainment Book.

An annual family membership to all three museums (Duke Energy Children's Museum, Museum of Natural History and Science, and Cincinnati History Museum) with free parking and free or discounted admission to 200+ museums worldwide is $130. We highly recommend this option.

Ages: 2 and up

Stroller and wheelchair friendly: Yes

Length of visit: 2–4 hours

Description and comments:

The Museum of Natural History and Science is a wonderful place to take kids of all ages. The older they get, the deeper they delve into the exhibits. Upon entering the museum, stop at the Information Desk to pick up the monthly scavenger hunt. For each question they answer correctly, kids earn points to spend in the Nature's Trading Post. They can also bring in items like rocks and seeds to trade in for points. Check the website for guidelines.

Do not miss the LITE Lab, where kids perform hands-on experiments. LITE stands for Learning, Innovation, Technology, and Education. Experiments vary so your kids can investigate something new each visit. In Earth Stories, watch an interactive program about Native American earthworks and a film about the planets. See a replica of Neil Armstrong's spacesuit.

Kids love the cave exhibit, a reproduction of a limestone cave, complete with stalactites and stalagmites, a waterfall, and an underground stream. Explore one of the two paths through the cave, one that is suitable for strollers and wheelchairs, and a more adventurous route with stairs. Kids love to wiggle through tunnels and weave through different passageways. Look for the live bats and learn about other animals that live in caves.

Another favorite is the Ice Age exhibit. Examine pollen through a microscope and discover what you can learn about animals that lived long ago by inspecting their bones. Older kids use computers to create a virtual ice age animal and prevent an animal from becoming extinct. They can test their knowledge with questions on lift-up panels. Our kids gravitate to a water and sand table where they can witness how water from glaciers sculpts the landscape. Make sure you point out the cross-section of a California Redwood to your kids and explain how you can determine the age of the tree when it was cut down by counting the rings. This one was almost 1,400 years old! Trek through the ice cave and walk amongst models of animals of the ice age, including an elk, bison, mastodon, and sloth.

Finally, learn about fossils, extinction, and dinosaurs. Dinosaur-loving kids will be fascinated by the dinosaur models and skeletons. Take a closer look to see which bones are real and which were cast. Check out the dinosaur room with a play table, dinosaur film, and lots of books. The museum also has a variety of daily demonstrations and many free scheduled activities. Check the website and the Information Desk for more information.

NATIONAL UNDERGROUND RAILROAD FREEDOM CENTER

Address: 50 E. Freedom Way, Cincinnati, OH 45202

Phone: (513) 333-7500
            (877) 648-4838

Website: www.freedomcenter.org

Hours: Tuesday–Saturday: 11 a.m.–5 p.m.

Cost: $12 Adults
            $10 Students (13–21)
            $8 Children (6–12)
            Free Children 5 and under, with paying adult
            $10 Seniors

            Check for AAA discount.

Ages: 8 and up

Stroller and wheelchair friendly: Yes

Length of visit: 2 hours

Description and comments:

The National Underground Railroad Freedom Center tells the important history of the underground resistance to slavery and the network of courageous people who risked their lives to help slaves escape. Learn how slaves were brought to the United States and how they were traded within the United States. One exhibit is an actual slave pen used by a Kentucky slave trader to hold slaves while moving them to slave markets. Go inside it and look for where the chains were attached. Most of the exhibits are beyond the understanding of younger children who may not comprehend the concept of slavery. The museum has created a complimentary audio tour designed for families and children. Your kids can identify the points on the tour and enter the corresponding number into the device and hold it up to their ear like a telephone to hear the commentary. They can listen to stories from the perspectives of both a young slave woman and a slave owner. The films are also a good choice for kids, especially *Brothers of the Borderland* because it helps them picture how the Underground Railroad operated.

NEUSOLE GLASSWORKS

Address: 656 E. McMillan Drive, Cincinnati, OH 45206

Phone: (513) 751-3292

Website: www.neusoleglassworks.com

Hours: By appointment

Cost: $8 per person for demonstrations
            $15 and up per person for workshops,
            depending on piece

Ages: 8 and up

Stroller and wheelchair friendly: Yes

Length of visit: 1–2 hours

Description and comments:

Neusole Glassworks is a not-for-profit organization dedicated to preserving the art of glassblowing. Their most basic offering is a glassblowing demonstration. For $8 per person, watch a skilled artist create a beautiful piece of glass art. It takes about an hour and the small group size allows for interaction with the artists. Visitors learn what a "glory hole" is used for and watch artists gather glass from a crucible in a furnace. It's amazing to watch the artists use a variety of tools and techniques to transform a molten blob of glass into a bowl, vase, or other art piece. During the demonstration, the artists discuss and answer questions about the process. We recommend this for ages 8 and up, or perhaps younger children if they have a long attention span.

Our favorite option at Neusole is the hands-on workshop. It includes a demonstration as described above, and then participants make their own project. A glass flower is an excellent choice for first timers. The artists outfit participants with gloves and tools and perform the more difficult tasks themselves. Participants are able to use the tools to stretch the glass into a flower shape. It's a fascinating and unforgettable experience! The finished pieces must be cooled very slowly in an annealing oven and picked up at a later date. Other workshop options include ornaments, pumpkins, and paperweights.

After the demonstration or workshop, visit the gallery which includes a rotating display from visiting artists. The adjacent gift shop has many pieces available for sale. If your workshop leaves you wanting to learn more, inquire about the more in-depth classes offered by Neusole.

NEWPORT AQUARIUM

Address: 1 Aquarium Way, Newport, KY 41071

Phone: (859) 261-7444

Website: www.newportaquarium.com

Hours: Daily: 10 a.m.–6 p.m.
            Extended hours during summer and holiday
            seasons. Check website for details.

Cost: $23 Adults
            $15 Children (2–12)
            Free Children 1 and under

            Annual passes are available for approximately
            the cost of two visits.

Ages: All ages

Stroller and wheelchair friendly: Strollers not permitted
during peak hours, but baby carriers and backpacks are
loaned free of charge. Check Stroller Calendar on website
for details.

Length of visit: 2 hours

Description and comments:

The Newport Aquarium has a variety of underwater
exhibits that appeal to all ages. On any given visit, you
might see a baby excitedly watching a turtle swim, a teenage
couple on a date, or older couples without children. When
you arrive, check the schedule to find out when there will
be shows in Shark Ray Bay. You won't want to miss hearing
scuba divers talk to you from inside the shark tank. There is
much for the shark lover to experience. It is surreal to watch
the sharks and shark rays swim right over your head as you

walk through an acrylic tunnel. In Shark Central, you can pet a shark as it swims by you. At the end of your visit, you are routed through an open-air viewing area where you can see the shark tank from above.

Other exhibits show the diversity of aquatic habitats, including a coral reef and river environments. Kids love to look at the fish and compare and contrast their colors, shapes, sizes, reflectivity, and other characteristics. Linger in the jellyfish exhibit and become mesmerized watching the pulsing jellyfish. Stroll down Gator Alley and visit Mighty Mike, the largest alligator in the country outside of Florida. He's 14 feet long and weighs 800 pounds! Watch the penguin show at Penguin Palooza. Informative videos are placed throughout the aquarium to help you learn more about the animals in the tanks. For a change of pace, stop by the Frog Bog where the kids climb and slide in the play area, play a video game, and learn from interactive exhibits.

The admission cost for the Newport Aquarium is pricier than most of the other Adventures in this book, but the annual pass is reasonably priced at approximately the cost of two visits. Discounts or coupons can often be found on their website and discounted tickets are sold at Kroger stores. The aquarium also offers additional programs for a fee, such as backstage animal experiences and penguin encounters.

PAUL BROWN STADIUM TOUR

Address: 1 Paul Brown Stadium, Cincinnati, OH 45202

Phone: (513) 455-4805

Website: www.bengals.com

Hours: April–mid-July
            Monday–Friday: 10 a.m.–2 p.m.

            Advance reservations required

Cost: $6 Adults
            $4 Children (3–18)
            Free Children 2 and under
            $4 Seniors

Ages: 5 and up

Stroller and wheelchair friendly: Yes

Length of visit: 1–2 hours

Description and comments:

Have you ever wondered what goes on behind the scenes at a Cincinnati Bengals game? The Paul Brown Stadium tour takes visitors into the stadium to satisfy the curiosity of football fans.

The tour begins in the Pro Shop where you can purchase your ticket and a plethora of Bengals gear. Bring cash, your check book, or your ATM card as credit cards are not accepted for the tour. The stops on the tour vary depending on the use of the stadium or the field. The tour takes you into a luxury suite and the West Club Lounge, which is available to season ticket holders and club seat ticket holders during games. Venture into the Press Box and pretend you are reporting on the game. You'll see the entrance to the Bengals locker room, but since you never know when it's being used, entering the locker room is off limits. Instead, the tour takes you into the visiting team's locker room. Finally, take in the stadium from the players' perspective when the tour heads to the football field. Run on the turf and pretend to kick a field goal. This is usually the highlight of the day for most kids.

Tours must be scheduled in advance. Stadium tours run only during the Bengals off-season which is generally April to mid-July. Summer is the busiest season for Paul Brown Stadium tours, so if you are looking to secure a particular date, it's best to reserve it early. Call anytime after the first of the year to schedule your tour.

PURPLE PEOPLE BRIDGE
(official name is the Newport Southbank Bridge)

Address: Over the Ohio River between Pete Rose Way in Cincinnati and Third Street in Newport

Phone: (859) 655-7700

Website: www.purplepeoplebridge.com

Ages: All ages

Stroller and wheelchair friendly: Yes

Length of visit: 1 hour (allow time for other attractions)

Description and comments:

Yes, it's a purple bridge. Why purple? Because that's what color focus groups picked when it was restored. This pedestrian bridge was previously the L&N Railroad Bridge.

This pedestrian-only bridge is just over a half-mile long and takes you from Newport to Cincinnati with a carefree walk. Lanes are present for bikers, walkers, and skaters. There are also park benches, handrails, security cameras, emergency call boxes, and trash cans on the bridge.

Combine a walk on the Purple People Bridge with a visit to Sawyer Point (see separate listing), Great American Ballpark or Paul Brown Stadium, dinner at a downtown restaurant, Newport on the Levee, or ice cream at Fountain Square. This bridge is a unique part of the Cincinnati/Northern Kentucky area.

A private company used to offer a Purple People Bridge Climb. Visitors could climb the catwalk over the bridge. Please note that this is no longer offered as an attraction.

RAILWAY MUSEUM OF GREATER CINCINNATI

Address: 315 W. Southern Avenue, Covington, KY 41015

Website: www.cincirailmuseum.org

Hours: Saturday: 10 a.m.–4 p.m.

Cost: $4 Adults
             $2 Children (10 and under)
             Groups larger than 12 should contact the
             museum office

Ages: 3 and up

Stroller and wheelchair friendly: No

Length of visit: 1–2 hours

Description and comments:

   The Railway Museum of Greater Cincinnati is a life-sized train museum. There are no model trains here: it's a genuine railroad yard with actual train cars. Leave the stroller at home. The train yard has tracks and contains many obstacles. Junior engineers view Pullman cars from 1911–1929 and sit at the controls of a Diesel locomotive. An overnight train includes a locomotive, post office, baggage, sleeping, and observation cars. Train lovers will be thrilled to stroll along the tracks and examine these cars up close. Museum volunteers are available and willing to answer questions. Upon entering, you'll receive a walking tour map to help you navigate the museum. A shaded picnic area is located on the property.

RIDE THE DUCKS – NEWPORT

Address: 1 Aquarium Way, Newport, KY 41071

Phone: (859) 815-1439

Website: www.newportducks.com

Hours: Approximately mid-March through October or November, depending on weather

Typically four tours are scheduled on weekdays and 7–8 tours per day on weekends

Check website for details

Cost: $17 Adults
$12 Children (2–12)
Free Children 1 and under, but ticket required

Ages: All

Stroller and wheelchair friendly: Wheelchairs are permitted, but require advance arrangements. Strollers are not permitted on board, but can be stowed near the departure site.

Length of visit: 45-minute tour

Description and comments:

There are many ways to tour a city, but we think an amphibious vehicle tour is ideal for our river city. Ride the Ducks has been offering Cincinnati tours since 2008. The vehicles are essentially a truck enclosed in a water-tight shell and were first used by the military in World War II. They drive on land, then drive into the water and operate as a boat. The 45-minute tour highlights landmarks in Cincinnati and Newport, with nuggets of history mixed in with the fun. Everyone on board is given a souvenir quacker and is encouraged to use it to quack at passers-by, a duck boat tradition. The ducks depart from Newport on the Levee, cross a bridge into Cincinnati, and drive to Cincinnati Public Landing for the exciting splashdown into the Ohio River. On the river you'll see the waterfront areas of Cincinnati, Newport, and Covington, including a unique view of the Roebling Murals (page 75), painted on the flood walls of Covington. The tour continues on land through the streets of Cincinnati and Newport. This is a fun way to learn more about the history of the area!

Tickets can be purchased in advance on their website. We recommend calling to confirm tour times. The Coast Guard will not allow the tours to operate if the river level is too low or too high. Pick up your tickets at the Newport on the Levee Welcome Center located on the plaza outside the Newport Aquarium. The tours depart from Third Street, near Brio Restaurant.

ROBERT D. LINDNER FAMILY OMNIMAX THEATER AT CINCINNATI MUSEUM CENTER

Address: 1301 Western Avenue, Cincinnati, OH 45203

Phone: (513) 287-7000
            (800) 733-2077

Website: www.cincymuseum.org

Hours: Monday–Saturday: 10 a.m.–5 p.m.
            Sunday: 11 a.m.–6 p.m.

Cost: $7.50 Adults
            $5.50 Children (3–12)
            $6.50 Seniors (60+)

            Discounts are offered if you visit a museum in addition to seeing an OMNIMAX film. Check website for more information.

Ages: 3 and up

Stroller and wheelchair friendly: Yes

Length of visit: 1 hour

Description and comments:

This OMNIMAX Theater is located at the Cincinnati Museum Center at Union Terminal. See high quality, family-friendly documentaries on the five-story, 72-foot diameter, tilted, domed screen. Pair this movie with one of the other museums for a discounted price. Be sure to check the website for available show titles and times. Tickets can be purchased online or at the Museum Center. Weekend shows sometimes sell out so it may be helpful to buy your tickets in advance. Please note that smaller children might be frightened by the intensity of the enormous screen and loud noises.

ROEBLING MURALS

Address: Roebling Suspension Bridge, Riverside Drive
            and Roebling Way, Covington, KY 41017

Hours: Always open

Cost: Free

Ages: All ages

Stroller and wheelchair friendly: Yes

Length of visit: 1 hour

Description and comments:

The Roebling Murals are located at the Covington Waterfront along the flood wall just west of the Roebling Suspension Bridge. They contain a series of 18 panels depicting the history of the Covington area from about 800 BC through 2008. This remarkable piece of art is a delightful gem that is hidden in plain sight. Many Cincinnati area residents are not aware that the murals exist. The murals were painted by Robert Dafford who has also painted murals in Maysville and Paducah, Kentucky; Camden, New Jersey; and Vicksburg, Mississippi.

The murals are impressive and beautifully painted. While visiting the murals, it is interesting to view them from a few feet away to notice all the intricate details. After looking at all the murals, step back about 20 feet and note the difference as you appreciate the depth and scale of the paintings. Trompe l'oeil technique is used to make the flat wall appear to be a three-dimensional stone wall. Kids are amused at how this technique creates the illusion that a young child is standing on a ledge pointing at one of the scenes.

In the murals you will see images of different time periods throughout the history of Kentucky. The first image is *The Great Buffalo Road*, a depiction of a herd of bison crossing the Ohio River around 800 BC. Further down the timeline is *The Flight of the Garner Family*. This is the story of a runaway slave family trying to reach freedom by crossing the Ohio River. *German Heritage* celebrates the German heritage and influence throughout the Covington area. *Play Ball* showcases the Covington Blue Sox baseball team that played in the early 1900's. There are murals illustrating the story of Daniel Carter Beard, who founded the Boy Scouts, The Flood of 1937, and other points in history up through a scene from the modern day riverfront. Look for a box containing information sheets near the murals. It's helpful to read the explanation of the murals while admiring each work of art.

SAWYER POINT & YEATMAN'S COVE

Address: 801 E. Pete Rose Way, Cincinnati, OH 45202

Phone: (513) 352-6180

Website: www.cincinnatiparks.com/index.php/sawyer-
           point-yeatman

Hours: Daily: 6 a.m.–11 p.m.

Cost: Free
           $2 Parking in Sawyer Point Lot

Ages: All ages

Stroller and wheelchair friendly: Yes

Length of visit: 2–4 hours

Description and comments:

   Sawyer Point is a mile-long park along the banks of the
Ohio River just south of downtown Cincinnati. The park has
loads of things to do; this could be a whole day's Adventure.
Starting out, the kids will love 1,000 Hands playground,
one of the best playgrounds in the area. Volunteers built
this playground in just six days in 2003. It was specifically
constructed so all kids could play together, including
those in wheelchairs. The playground sits under the Big
Mac Bridge (the yellow, arched bridge) so it provides lots
of shade and protection from rain. The floor of the entire
playground is covered with soft rubber flooring to keep
the kids safe from injuries. Ramps and handicap accessible
swings are also on hand. Zip lines, sandboxes, tire swings,
towers, monkey bars, and slides add to the excitement, too.

   Sawyer Point includes volleyball courts, tennis courts,
and bike rentals. Several maps and signs throughout the

park explain the history of Cincinnati and the river as a riverboat port, as part of the Miami-Erie Canal, and as a major industrial center. Stroll the River Walk and admire the statue of Cincinnati's namesake, Roman hero Lucius Quinctius Cincinnatus, welcoming you to Sawyer Point. The flood column on the statue marks the levels of the three great floods, including the 1937 flood that reached heights of almost 80 feet and devastated the surrounding area.

The Serpentine Wall is another favorite feature of Sawyer Point. The wall follows the river and has large curvy stair steps along the river bank. Climbing up and down the steps can keep kids happily entertained for quite a while. Watch the boats on the river and stroll down to Great American Ballpark, the home of the Cincinnati Reds. Admire the National Steamboat Monument at the Public Landing. It holds a 60-ton replica paddle wheel and steam is released every minute from the tall stacks.

Wander westward down the street and you'll find Concourse Fountain and Sprayground; a wet playground where the kids can cool off. This is located between the parking lots at Sawyer Point and the Public Landing. You'll have to walk to get there from either lot, so you might want to take a stroller. Remember to pack swimsuits, sunscreen, and towels for the kids.

SKY GALLEY RESTAURANT
AT LUNKEN AIRPORT

Address: 262 Wilmer Avenue, Cincinnati, OH 45226

Phone: (513) 871-7400

Website: www.skygalley.com

Hours: Sunday–Thursday: 11 a.m.–9 p.m.
Friday and Saturday: 11 a.m.–10 p.m.

Cost: $7–$10 sandwiches
$9–$12 salads
$13–$23 entrees
$4.95 Kids' menu

Ages: All ages

Stroller and wheelchair friendly: Yes

Length of visit: 1–2 hours

Description and comments:

The Sky Galley's big draw is its view—airplanes taking off and landing at Lunken Airport. The airport now serves private airplanes and corporate jets, but at its dedication in 1930 it was the largest municipal airport in the world. Sky Galley is located inside the airport terminal and, before it was converted into a restaurant, meals were prepared there for flights on American Airlines. You may dine indoors or out on the patio and the kids will be fascinated watching the planes. The prices are reasonable and there is a kids' menu with the typical choices (burgers, grilled cheese sandwiches, chicken tenders, etc.) available for $4.95 including beverage. Reservations are recommended, especially for large groups. Ask for a table with a good view of the planes.

ST. MARY'S CATHEDRAL BASILICA OF THE ASSUMPTION

Address: 1140 Madison Avenue, Covington, KY 41011

Phone: (859) 431-2060

Website: www.covcathedral.com
             www.cathedralconcertseries.org

Hours: Monday–Saturday: 9:30 a.m.–4 p.m.
             Mass held at 9:30 a.m.

Cost: Donations appreciated

Ages: 10 and up

Stroller and wheelchair friendly: Yes

Length of visit: 1 hour

Description and comments:

You don't need to travel to Europe to see a beautiful cathedral; just head to Covington. A visit to St. Mary's Cathedral Basilica of the Assumption will make you feel as if you've been transported to Paris. The façade of St. Mary's was inspired by Notre Dame in Paris, but it's just one-third the size, and it boasts one of the largest stained glass windows in the world. Visitors come from all over the world to see this architectural gem.

Tours are self-guided, though we found that the people working were happy to answer questions and point out interesting features. Groups of ten or more should call in advance and schedule a guided tour. This tour is best for older kids and adults. The most notable feature of the cathedral is the colossal stained glass window, which measures 67 feet high and 24 feet wide. There are 81 smaller windows in the cathedral that depict Jesus as a child, Jesus as an adult, apostles and early Christians, miracles of Christ, and the seven sacraments. Perhaps even more beautiful than the stained glass windows, and easier for kids to see, are the mosaic stations of the cross. Created in Venice in 1915, these mosaic masterpieces each contain as many as 80,000 tiles and are replicas of oil paintings. All of the tiles are made of porcelain ceramic, except one. In the station where Jesus is removed from the cross, Mary is at his side and a single teardrop created from mother-of-pearl falls from her eye. Challenge your kids to see if they can find it. Other artistic touches in the cathedral include a carved marble baptistry, murals, statues, and intricately carved wood pieces in the sanctuary.

The Cathedral Basilica contains not one, but three pipe organs. The best way to hear them is to attend a performance during the Concert Series season which runs from October through April. The concerts are open to the public and have no admission charge although an offering is taken. Concerts are at 3 p.m. on Sunday afternoons and feature instrumental and choral music with guest musicians, ensembles, and choruses. These concerts are a wonderful way to appreciate the grandeur of the Cathedral. The most kid-friendly of the concerts is the Epiphany Epilogue concert, celebrating the end of the Christmas season.

SUNROCK FARM

Address: 103 Gibson Lane, Wilder, KY 41076

Phone: (859) 781-5502

Website: www.sunrockfarm.org

Hours: By reservation only
Open every day except Christmas and
New Years Day

Cost: $10 Adults and children (Cash only)

Ages: 2–18

Stroller and wheelchair friendly: Gravel or grass paths, large-wheeled strollers are best

Length of visit: 2 hours

Description and comments:

Do you have a young farmer or animal lover in your family? Sunrock Farm will provide a tour of their farm to groups of 8–10 people. They may be able to match you up with another family or two if you don't have enough people for a tour. The tour provides several hands-on experiences including milking a goat, holding baby chicks, gathering eggs, bottle feeding baby sheep or goats (if they are available), brushing horses, and visiting the oxen, emu, and alpaca. Plenty of great photo opportunities are available. Your kids will understand how the farm works, while seeing and touching the animals. Portable restrooms and hand-washing stations are available. Picnic tables are available for school groups, but not family groups.

TOTTER'S OTTERVILLE

Address: 4314 Boron Drive, Covington, KY 41015

Phone: (859) 491-1441

Website: www.tottersotterville.com

Hours: Monday–Thursday: 10 a.m.–5 p.m.
Friday and Saturday: 10 a.m.–8 p.m.
Sunday: 11 a.m.–5 p.m.
Closed some holidays

Cost: $7.95 Children 1 and up
Free Children under 1
Free Adults
Annual passes and value passes available

Ages: 8 and under

Stroller and wheelchair friendly: Yes

Length of visit: 2–4 hours

Description and comments:

Choose from over 25 fun and educational activities both indoors and outdoors. Outside you'll find a train to ride on, squirting fire hydrants, a maze, and a fishing area with magnetic fish. Dig for dinosaur bones or work on a construction site. Inside are several areas for creative and pretend play. A special area for kids under age three contains soft and colorful toys. Dress-up clothes are provided for kids to pretend they are ballerinas, construction workers, or a variety of other people. Play with the train sets and climb on the multi-level play set.

TOWER A AT CINCINNATI UNION TERMINAL

Address: 1301 Western Avenue, Cincinnati, OH 45203

Phone: (513) 287-7000

Website: www.cincymuseum.org/node/1611

Hours: Wednesday–Sunday: Noon–4 p.m.

Cost: Free

Ages: 3 and up

Stroller and wheelchair friendly: No

Length of visit: 1 hour

Description and comments:

Do you have a train enthusiast in your family? Young fans of Thomas the Tank Engine™, long-time model train collectors, or anyone interested in the history of transportation will enjoy a trip up to Tower A. Tower A is located in the Cincinnati Museum Center, back towards the Omnimax Theater entrance. A stairway takes you up to the tower, so it is not handicap or stroller accessible.

Tower A is the former Control Room of Union Terminal. This is where the controllers watched over all the incoming and outgoing buses and trains carrying countless people and cargo daily. It has been restored and is maintained and staffed by the Cincinnati Railroad Club. The enthusiastic and knowledgeable volunteers are available to explain the history of the tower and answer any questions you might have. The Tower contains the old desk where the controllers once sat high above the train tracks to oversee the activity in the train yard below. The map of the train tracks on the wall shows how the controllers could see where trains were as their locations lit up on this map. Displays showcase many of the historical artifacts, pictures, and documents of the activity of the control room.

The large windows in the control room overlook the train tracks that are still in use today. Large machines pick up containers off of the trains and carefully place them on the tractor trailers to be hauled to their next destination. It is fascinating to watch the precision of these machines when moving these large containers.

Tower A contains a gift shop, a train library, train memorabilia, and also train tables for the kids to play with. Be sure to stop in next time you are visiting the Cincinnati Museum Center but take note of the limited hours of Tower A.

UNMUSEUM AT THE
CONTEMPORARY ARTS CENTER

Address: 44 E. 6th Street, Cincinnati, OH 45202

Phone: (513) 345-8400

Website: www.contemporaryartscenter.org/unmuseum

Hours: Monday: 10 a.m.–9 p.m.
            (5–9 p.m. free admission)
            Tuesday: Closed
            Wednesday–Friday: 10 a.m.–6 p.m.
            Saturday and Sunday: 11 a.m.–6 p.m.

Cost: $7.50   Adults
            $5.50   Children (5 and up)
            Free Children 4 and under
            $5.50 Seniors (65+)
            Free admission on Mondays from 5–9 p.m.

            Check for AAA discount.

Ages: 3 and up

Stroller and wheelchair friendly: Yes

Length of visit: 1–2 hours

Description and comments:

The UnMuseum at the Contemporary Arts Center is a place to explore art in an out-of-the-box sort of way. The entire 6th floor is filled with interactive exhibits for children. Some of the exhibits are musical exhibits and most of the exhibits are hands-on. In the Art Lab, which is stocked with art supplies, kids can create their own masterpiece. The fee includes admission to the entire center which has rotating exhibits, but we suggest asking if any areas might not be appropriate for children.

There are special programs for families and children. The fourth Sunday of every month from 1–4 p.m. is Family Sunday. An artist or educator helps families create an art project. These projects are designed for ages 5 and up. Thursday Art Play is held on the second and fourth Thursday of each month from 1–2 p.m. This program is geared for younger children, ages 3–7, and a parent. Both programs are free with museum admission. On the first Saturday of each month is a program called "44." Although 44 is not designed specifically for children, some of the presentations are very appealing to them. This free program is held in the lobby and does not require museum admission. Check the website for details on this and other family-friendly programs.

VENT HAVEN MUSEUM

<u>Address:</u>   33 West Maple Avenue, Fort Mitchell, KY 41011

<u>Phone:</u>   (859) 341-0461

<u>Website:</u>   www.venthavenmuseum.com

<u>Hours:</u>   May–September, by appointment. At least
        three days' notice is required.

<u>Cost:</u> $10 per person

<u>Ages:</u>   7 and up

<u>Stroller and wheelchair friendly:</u> Limited

<u>Length of visit:</u> 1 hour

<u>Description and comments:</u>

Did you know that Greater Cincinnati is home to the world's only ventriloquism museum? This little-known gem is located in Fort Mitchell, Kentucky. The museum was founded by Cincinnati native, William Shakespeare Berger, known as W.S. In 1910 he purchased his first dummy, Tommy Baloney, and began a collection that has since grown to over 800 dummies and puppets filling three buildings.

The museum is open May through September by appointment only, but don't let that prevent you from visiting. The museum's curator is very flexible with appointment times. She is able to schedule daytime or evening, weekend or weekday appointments and no minimum number of people is required. The tour length ranges from 45 to 90 minutes, depending on the interest of the group. You will learn about the history of ventriloquism and about the most well-known ventriloquists and their figures. The collection appeals to fans of all ages, so it's a perfect adventure to go on with kids and their grandparents.

The older generation will appreciate a replica of Edgar Bergen's Charlie McCarthy and Mortimer Snerd. People who grew up in the 1950's will remember Jimmy Nelson's Farfel the dog and Danny O'Day from Nestlé Quik commercials. Comedy fans will recognize Jeff Dunham's Walter, Jose Jalapeno, and Peanut. The puppets that are most likely to be familiar to kids are those that Terry Fator brought to life as singing impersonators on the reality television show, America's Got Talent: Emma Taylor and Winston, an adorable turtle. Other recognizable dummies include former presidents Ronald Reagan and Jimmy Carter. In addition to dummies and puppets, Vent Haven has plenty of memorabilia and photographs of ventriloquists.

Be aware that while dummies and puppets are appealing to kids, it is not a hands-on museum. Tell kids ahead of time that they will not be able to touch any of the dummies or puppets. Also, there are no public restrooms on site. Make sure you make a stop before you arrive at the museum. Flash photography is not permitted in the museum.

To request a tour, call or send an email to venthaven@ insightbb.com.

WILLIAM HOWARD TAFT
NATIONAL HISTORIC SITE

Address: 2038 Auburn Avenue, Cincinnati, OH 45219

Phone: (513) 684-3262

Website: www.nps.gov/wiho/index.htm

Hours: Daily: 8 a.m.–4:15 p.m.
            Closed some holidays

Cost: Free

Ages: 8 and up

Stroller and wheelchair friendly: Wheelchair accessible
Strollers not allowed in the house

Length of visit: 1 hour

Description and comments:

Visit the William Howard Taft Home and Taft Education Center for a glimpse into what life was like in the early days of our 27th President of the United States and the 10th Chief Justice of the United States. Learn the history of how his family came to Cincinnati, and how he came to be the only person to have held the two highest positions in the United States of America. Guided tours are available every half hour. Begin your tour in the Taft Education Center and meet an animatronic figure of Charles P. Taft II, the son of William Howard Taft. Charles talks to visitors about his interesting family. There is also an orientation video which will explain more about the Tafts' lives.

The tour takes you through Taft's childhood home. Each room on the first floor is decorated in period pieces as it would have been at the time the Tafts occupied it. See the sitting room, the children's room, the library, and several other rooms. The upstairs rooms have been filled with displays about the life of his parents, siblings, and children. You'll also find a menu of a dinner served at a White House party.

The rangers are extremely knowledgeable and answer all your questions. This Adventure is probably best for children 8 and older, but younger children might appreciate seeing the house that a former president lived in as a child. Request a free Junior Ranger booklet which your child can fill out during and after the tour. Upon completion, they present it to a ranger, receive a certificate and pin, and are sworn in as a Junior Ranger.

WORLD PEACE BELL

Address: 425 York Street (4th & York),
           Newport, KY 41071

Hours: Always open
           Bell swings at five minutes before Noon daily

Cost: Free

Ages: All ages

Stroller and wheelchair friendly: Yes

Length of visit: <1 hour

Description and comments:

The World Peace Bell is 12 feet tall and 12 feet wide and weighs 66,000 pounds. It is the world's largest free-swinging bell and first swung to ring in the year 2000. It swings daily at five minutes before Noon. The bell was created by The Verdin Company and was cast in France. The bell is VERY loud, but kids can cover their ears and be entertained. You can stand directly underneath it and see the clapper strike the bell.

GREATER CINCINNATI

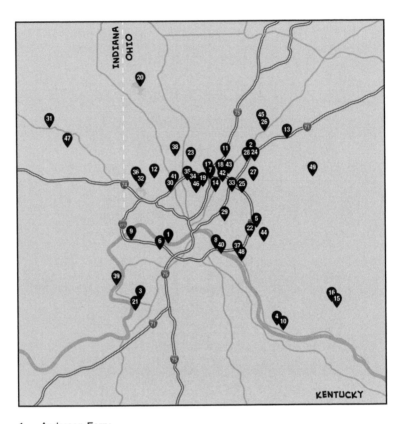

1   Anderson Ferry

2   The Beach Waterpark

3   Big Bone Lick State Park

4   Chilo Lock 34 Park

5   Cincinnati Nature Center - Rowe Woods

6   Cincinnati/Northern Kentucky International Airport

7   CoCo Key Water Resort

8   Coney Island

9   Creation Museum

10   Crooked Run Nature Preserve

11   EnterTRAINment Junction

12   Fernald Preserve

13   Fort Ancient

14   Gorman Heritage Farm

15   Grant Boyhood Home

16   Grant Schoolhouse

17   Hands Against Hunger at the Hope Factory

18   Heritage Village Museum at Sharon Woods

19   Highfield Discovery Garden at Glenwood Gardens

20   Hueston Woods State Park

21   Jane's Saddlebag

22   Jungle Jim's International Market - Eastgate

23   Jungle Jim's International Market - Fairfield

24   Kings Island and Soak City Waterpark

25   Lake Isabella

26   Lebanon Mason Monroe Railroad

27   Little Miami Bike Trail

28   Loveland Castle - Chateau LaRoche

29   Mariemont Bell Tower Carillon

30   Megaland at Colerain Park

31   Metamora, Indiana

32   Miami Whitewater Forest

33   OZO Play Café

34   Parky's Farm at Winton Woods

35   Parky's Wet Playground - Parky's Ark at Winton Woods

36   Parky's Wet Playground - Parky's Pirate Cove at Miami Whitewater Forest

37   Parky's Wet Playground - Parky's Wetland Adventure at Woodland Mound

38   Pyramid Hill Sculpture Park & Museum

39   Rabbit Hash, Kentucky

40   River Downs

41   Rumpke Landfill Tour

42   Sharon Woods

43   Trammel Fossil Park

44   Tri State Warbird Museum

45   Warren County History Center and Glendower

46   Winton Woods

47   Wolf Creek Habitat

48   Woodland Mound

49   World's Largest Horseshoe Crab

See Central Cincinnati and Northern Kentucky Map for additional attractions.

ANDERSON FERRY

Address: Anderson Ferry Road and Route 50 in Ohio
            4030 River Road, Constance, KY 41048

Phone: (859) 586-5007

Website: andersonferryofficial.com

Hours: May–October
            Monday–Friday: 6 a.m.–9:45 p.m.
            Saturday: 7 a.m.–9:45 p.m.
            Sunday: 9 a.m.–9:45 p.m.

            November–April
            Monday–Friday: 6 a.m.–8 p.m.
            Saturday: 7 a.m.–8 p.m.
            Sunday: 10 a.m.–8 p.m.

Cost: $5 per car one way
            $7 round trip

Ages: All ages

Stroller and wheelchair friendly: Yes

Length of visit: <1 hour

Description and comments:

The Anderson Ferry has continuously transported vehicles across the Ohio River since 1817 and is on the National Register of Historic Places. In its early days, horses on each side of the river powered the boat. Although not really a destination in itself, this is a unique way for kids to experience crossing the river. This is ideal to work into your schedule if you are traveling somewhere close to the airport or the ferry. Arrive anytime during operating hours and they will quickly transport you across the river. Drive your car right onto the boat and enjoy the short ride. The ferry workers often feed the ducks and sometimes a duck will hop on board for a ride. See if your kids can spot any hitchhiking ducks.

Riding the ferry helps children understand how people crossed the river before there were bridges. This adventure may seem simple, but becomes something special through the eyes of a child. Be sure to carry cash or purchase your ticket online ahead of time because credit cards are not accepted.

THE BEACH WATERPARK

Address: 2590 Water Park Drive, Mason, OH 45040

Phone: (513) 398-7946

Website: www.thebeachwaterpark.com

Hours: Mid-May–mid-September
Check website for hours

Cost: $29.99 Adults and children over 45"
$14.99 Children (under 45")
Free Children 3 and under

Check website for online prices
and special packages.

Ages: All ages

Stroller and wheelchair friendly: Yes

Length of visit: 2 hours–all day

Description and comments:

The Beach Waterpark recently reopened under new ownership with new attractions. Big Creek Beach features a 600-gallon dump bucket, water cannons, and four small slides. Lil' Kahunas Waterworks allows toddlers to play in fountains and sprays sized just for them. Children need to be 45" to ride the big waterslides. Be careful in the Kokomo Lazy River with your smaller children; they may be safer riding with you if it is too deep for them to touch the bottom. Grab a complimentary tube and ride the waves with your family in the wave pool. A favorite spot is Paradise Cove, an 80-degree spa-pool where you can relax in the warm water.

Older kids love the many thrilling slides available in the

park. The Cliff has been rated one of the top water slides in the country and drops you five stories in three seconds! The many swift and steep water slides keep them busy all day.

Picnic tables are available outside the park if you want to pack your lunch. Guests are not permitted to bring outside food into the park. Plenty of concession stands are available with snacks, drinks, and meals. Mornings are least crowded at The Beach. After lunch the crowds generally grow larger.

BIG BONE LICK STATE HISTORIC SITE

Address: 3380 Beaver Road, Union, KY 41091

Phone: (859) 384-3522

Website: www.parks.ky.gov/parks/historicsites/big-
            bone-lick

Hours: Grounds:
            Open daily, year round, during daylight hours

            Visitor's center:
            April–December
            Daily: 9 a.m.–4 p.m.

Cost: Free entrance to park, visitor center,
            and outdoor museum

Ages: All ages

Stroller and wheelchair friendly: Yes

Length of visit: 2 hours

Description and comments:

Big Bone Lick was the location of many fossil finds of large Ice Age animals such as mammoths and mastodons, discovered in 1789 and displayed at museums throughout the world. Now it is a place to learn about the animals that once roamed the area. According to paleontologists, during the Pleistocene Epoch, when ice covered much of North America, prehistoric animals were attracted to the warm salt springs, where they became trapped and perished. Walk along a paved trail through an outdoor museum with recreated grasslands and wetlands and a life-size diorama of a bog. Other trails allow visitors to see the last remaining salt-sulphur spring and a herd of bison that kids find fascinating.

The visitor center contains a small museum with displays of fossilized bones and artifacts which provide clues about life in prehistoric Kentucky. The park offers a variety of other recreational facilities including picnic tables and grills, a playground, basketball court, horseshoes, miniature golf, and a swimming pool. A recreation staff conducts activities Memorial Day through Labor Day. A fishing lake and a campground with camp store are also on site.

CHILO LOCK 34 PARK

<u>Address:</u>   521 County Park Road, Chilo, OH 45112

<u>Phone:</u>   (513) 876-9013

<u>Website:</u>   www.clermontparks.org / Chilo.aspx

<u>Hours:</u>   Hours very by season. Call or check website

<u>Cost:</u>   Free

<u>Ages:</u>   All ages

<u>Stroller and wheelchair friendly:</u> Yes

<u>Length of visit:</u> 2 hours

<u>Description and comments:</u>

Chilo Lock 34 Park is located on the site of a former lock and dam on the Ohio River. The visitor's center and museum explain the history of both the Ohio River and the system of locks and dams which were vital to this area. The museum has kid-friendly displays covering nature and the locks. Hear different steamboat whistles or use a handcrank to operate a model of a lock. A kids' "Touch Table" allows kids to touch objects from nature including animal skins, bones, and seed pods. Another display features stuffed wildlife. The outdoor observation deck provides a great view of the Ohio River where you can watch barges and other boats float past you. With informative plaques placed around the park, the self-guided walking tour is great for older children and adults. Be on the lookout for wildlife in the 1.5-acre wetland here. The park also boasts a steamboat-themed playground and picnic shelters. You will be taught the importance of the locks in the history of the river while experiencing the nature surrounding the area. Combine this visit with a hike in the adjacent Crooked Run Nature Preserve. (See listing on page 114.)

CINCINNATI NATURE CENTER – ROWE WOODS

Address: 4949 Tealtown Road, Milford, OH 45150

Phone: (513) 831-1711

Website: www.cincynature.org

Hours: Open daily
            Hours vary by season but grounds always
            open at 8 a.m.

Cost: $8 Adults
            $3 Children (3–12)
            $6 Seniors (65+)

Ages: All ages

Stroller and wheelchair friendly: Yes

Length of visit: 2–4 hours

Description and comments:

Cincinnati Nature Center is a beautiful, natural oasis in the Cincinnati suburbs. There are 1,025 acres of land with ponds, meadows, forests, hills, and streams. The Nature Center includes 16 miles of well-marked hiking trails of varying length and difficulty, including one appropriate for strollers and wheelchairs. The visitor's center provides trail maps to help you explore the area. While in the visitor's center, request an adventure backpack containing tools for junior naturalists to investigate their surroundings. Hike the Edge Trail along the boardwalk on the edge of the pond. Remember to bring quarters for fish and turtle food. Wander along the path to Lotus Pond or Matt's Pond during the spring and summer to discover the giant bull frogs. Tread softly along the edge of the pond and try to spot the frogs before they hop into the water. Visit the historic log cabin and try to figure out which side was built most recently. Look for raccoons, deer, snakes, owls, and lots and lots of birds. Take advantage of one of several bird blinds along the trails, where you can watch the birds without them seeing you. The Marge & Charles Schott Nature PlayScape is a must for younger kids and encourages unstructured play amidst the elements of nature. Expect kids to get dirty and bring a change of clothes. Enjoy your lunch outside at a picnic table or at tables inside the Nature Center library.

Each season provides something special at Rowe Woods. During the spring admire thousands of daffodils in bloom. As summer arrives, the leaves take over and change the look of the woods. Fall, of course, brings beautiful changes of colors, and winter is a fun time to bundle up (pack your boots) and hike while searching for wildlife.

Inside the Nature Center you'll find several interesting displays. Listen to various bird calls, see the length of an eagle's wing span, and understand the life and trials of migratory birds. Your children can engage in interactive exhibits, climb through a hollow log, and draw a picture for all to see. Visit live snakes, toads, fish, and spiders on display too. Use the binoculars to admire the birds through the large viewing window and try to identify them. A gift shop has a nice selection of books, jewelry, hiking supplies, and nature-inspired art.

If you have questions about nature, animals, trees, birds, etc., be sure to ask one of the naturalists. They are extremely knowledgeable and happy to help.

CINCINNATI/NORTHERN KENTUCKY INTERNATIONAL AIRPORT TOUR

Address: 2939 Terminal Drive, Hebron, KY 41048

Phone: (859) 767-3144

Website: www.cvgairport.com/about/tours.aspx

Hours: By appointment on the 2nd and 3rd Wednesdays and 3rd Saturday of the month

Cost: Free tour
Free parking

Ages: 5 and up

Stroller and wheelchair friendly: No

Length of visit: Tour lasts 90 minutes; allow extra time to play at park and watch planes

Description and comments:

You'll need to gather a group of at least 15 people and call at least two weeks in advance in order to take a tour of the Cincinnati/Northern Kentucky International Airport, but you will be glad you did. You will tour the airfield to see operations up close. Your tour will include a visit to the airport fire department where kids learn about special equipment and training needed to fight airplane fires. The tour does not include baggage handling or airport operations, but the kids on our tour had a great time. Holscher Park is on the airport grounds and has a shelter, picnic tables, a play runway, and plenty of room for the kids to run around. Make sure everyone uses the restroom before you leave the airport because there are no restrooms at the park. Another interesting stop on the airport grounds is the Airport

Viewing Area, located near 1533 Donaldson Highway, near the intersection with Mineola Pike. It is open from 8 a.m. until 10 p.m. every day and provides an excellent view of planes taking off and landing.

COCO KEY WATER RESORT

Address: 11320 Chester Road, Cincinnati, OH 45246

Phone: (513) 771-2080

Website: www.cocokeycincinnati.com

Hours: Always open Thursday–Sunday
Open Monday–Wednesday seasonally
Hours vary seasonally. Check website for
details.

Cost: Day pass rates average $25 per person. Rates
can be higher on peak days and lower at other
times. Check website for online specials.
Children 1 and under are free.

Ages: 0–12

Stroller and wheelchair friendly: Strollers and wheelchairs
are permitted in the resort, but not in the water.

Length of visit: 4 hours–all day

Description and comments:

CoCo Key Water Resort is an indoor water park that
is sure to please the kids. It is attached to the Radisson
Cincinnati North hotel and offers either overnight packages
or day passes. There is a changing area with showers
and lockers and towels are provided. Swim diapers are
required. Young children gravitate toward Parrot's Perch
which has small slides, an umbrella water feature, a zero-
depth entry area, and water cannons. Watch out for the little
ones when the giant bucket spills over. The Dip-In Theater
shows animated movies or television programs on a boat
sail screen. Older kids (over 48″ tall) love the water slides.

There are two body slides and two tube slides. They have tubes for either one or two people. Coral Reef Cavern is an activity pool where kids play water basketball or cross the pool on lily pads. Float through the resort on a tube, on the lazy river ride. Palm Grotto is a hot tub that is designated for adults, but if the park isn't busy, they will allow kids to enter with an adult. The hot tub has a swim-through passage to the outdoor hot tub. CoCo Key also has a nice arcade area with video games and skee-ball, where kids collect tickets to trade in at the redemption area. There is a Pizza Hut Express and an A&W restaurant located inside the resort.

CONEY ISLAND

Address: 6201 Kellogg Avenue, Cincinnati, OH 45230

Phone: (513) 232-8230

Website: www.coneyislandpark.com

Hours: Daily, Memorial Day–Labor Day
Sunlite Pool: 10 a.m.–8 p.m.
Classic Rides: 11 a.m.–8 p.m.
Hours may vary. Check website for schedule.

Cost: Sunlite Pool:
$13.95 Adults and children 4+ ($8.95 after 4 p.m.)
$4.95 Children (2–3)

Coney's Classic Rides:
$11.95 All Day Ride Bracelet (4+)
($7.95 after 4 p.m.)
$6.95 All Day Ride Bracelet (3 and under)

No fee to walk around the park or see shows

Sunlite Pool & Classic Rides Combo Ticket
$23.95 Adults & children 4+ ($11.95 after 4 p.m.)
$10.95 Children (2–3)

$8 Parking

Check for AAA discount.

Ages: 2 and up

Stroller and wheelchair friendly: Yes

Length of visit: 2 hours–all day

Description and comments:

Founded on June 21, 1886, Coney Island is a Cincinnati tradition. Situated on 75 acres, Coney Island has more than 50 rides and attractions, including Sunlite Pool, the world's largest recirculating swimming pool. Splash around in over an acre of shallow water. The Twister waterslide attraction has two body slides and two double-innertube slides. Kids taller than 48″ can race each other down the Twister and zoom down the park's other three waterslides.

The other side of the park has 23 classic carnival-type rides, like the Scrambler, Ferris Wheel, and Tilt-A-Whirl. Adventurous riders should experience the thrill of a 50-foot freefall on The Scream Machine. Our kids love to hop on a mat and zip down the Giant Slide. Spend some time on the waters of Lake Como in a bumper boat, canoe, or pedal boat. Six rides have been designed specifically for young children under 48″ tall, including the Frog Hopper and Turtle Parade. Plan to watch at least one of several live stage shows that include music, singing, and dancing. Our kids love the audience participation in the kids' shows. Small children love exploring Coney Mining Town. You'll also find a miniature golf course and arcade games. Coney Island hosts several festivals and special events throughout the year. Check the website for details.

CREATION MUSEUM

Address: 2800 Bullittsburg Church Road,
             Petersburg, KY 41080

Phone: (888) 582-4253

Website: www.creationmuseum.org

Hours: Monday–Friday: 10 a.m.–6 p.m.
             Saturday: 9 a.m.–6 p.m.
             Sunday: Noon–6 p.m.

Cost: $29.95 Adults
             $15.95 Children (5–12)
             Free Children 4 and under
             $23.95 Seniors (60+)
             $7.95 Planetarium with admission

             Tickets include admission for two
             consecutive days

Ages: 5 and up

Stroller and wheelchair friendly: Yes

Length of visit: 2 hours–all day

Description and comments:

   The Creation Museum holds 165 displays filled with scientific evidence supporting the model of creation. The displays and films in this museum are state-of-the-art. Many of the animatronic displays were created by Patrick Marsh, who developed attractions like *Jaws* and *King Kong* at Universal Studios. Enter with an open mind and you will understand more about different ideas of how we all came to be. "Walk through Biblical History" is the main part of the museum. It is a self-guided tour including Adam and

Eve, Noah's Ark, and ending with Jesus. Walk on the life-sized model of a section of Noah's Ark. You can visit the Dinosaur Den (not handicapped accessible) and identify several dinosaurs along with a fossilized dinosaur egg, a triceratops skeleton casting, and a large allosaur skeleton.

You shouldn't miss the several professionally made films. The Stargazers Planetarium (for an additional fee) boasts digital technology and is a spectacular show you will enjoy in comfortable reclining seats. The Special Effects theater (no extra charge) was our kids' favorite show. This theater has vibrating seats and mist-spraying jets. The film about dragons and their place in both fairytales and biblical history is also intriguing.

Outside the museum is a delightful botanical garden with a mile of paved walking trails. Cross over five bridges and admire the blooming flowers and scenic waterfalls. A picnic area is available here, also. A restaurant is located inside the museum. Visit the petting zoo outside with a variety of animals including a camel, wallaby, goats, and many others. In 2013, the largest zip-line course in the Midwest was added, along with an aerial ropes course. Several packages with different lengths and prices are offered.

Between spending time inside the museum viewing the displays, watching the movies, having lunch, and journeying outside, a whole day (or two) of learning and fun is enjoyed by everyone.

CROOKED RUN NATURE PRESERVE

Address: 521 County Park Road, Chilo, OH 45112

Phone: (513) 732-2977

Website: www.clermontparks.org/Crooked.aspx

Hours: Open daily, year round, during daylight hours

Cost: Free

Ages: All ages

Stroller and wheelchair friendly: Trails are flat, but unpaved

Length of visit: 2 hours

Description and comments:

The Crooked Run Nature preserve sits next to Chilo Lock 34 Park. This is a beautiful park along the Ohio River. While hiking the property, observe the birds and animals through three wildlife viewing blinds. Visitors and staff have spotted over 190 types of birds in the park. Pack your binoculars and see what you can find. Kids might want to have a notebook or a bird identification book to record their observations. The park contains over one mile of hiking trails and has scenic overlooks of the river. Restroom and picnic facilities are available. The Naturalist's office is adjacent in Chilo Lock 34 Park. Check the website for scheduled programs. Tent-like yurts are available for overnight camping; reservations required.

ENTERTRAINMENT JUNCTION

Address: 7379 Squire Court, West Chester, OH 45069

Phone: (513) 898-8000
         (877) 898-4656

Website: www.entertrainmentjunction.com

Hours: Monday–Saturday: 10 a.m.–6 p.m.
         Sunday: Noon–6 p.m.

         Closed Wednesdays in January for
         maintenance

Cost: EnterTRAINment Journey
         $12.95 Adults
         $9.95 Children (3–12)
         Free Children 2 and under
         $11.50 Seniors (65+)

         A-Maze-N Funhouse
         $9.95 All Ages

         Seasonal attractions have additional fee; combo
         tickets available. Check website or AAA for
         discounts.

Ages: 2 and up

Stroller and wheelchair friendly: Yes

Length of visit: 2 hours

Description and comments:

   Train enthusiasts relish a visit to EnterTRAINment
Junction. Stroll through the world's largest indoor interactive
model train display, covering three periods of railroading.
Young children enjoy pushing buttons that trigger sound

effects or set a train into motion. Stop at the Imagination Junction—a play area with a climbing structure, wooden train table, and video screen showing *Thomas the Tank Engine* movies. In the American Railroading Museum, learn about the evolution of locomotives, railroad lore, and how railroads affected the American culture. A display shows the actual size of a train engine wheel, but the museum does not contain any actual railway cars. Test your knowledge at interactive kiosks. EnterTRAINment Junction also includes an expo center with additional train layouts and artifacts, seasonal attractions (for an additional fee), a café, and outdoor hand crank railroad cars that operate seasonally.

The A-Maze-N Funhouse was added in 2011. This funhouse lives up to its name with attractions like a mirror maze, curtain maze, and a claustrophobia hallway.

FERNALD PRESERVE

Address: 7400 Willey Road, Harrison, OH 45030

Phone: (513) 648-6000

Website: www.lm.doe.gov / Fernald / Visitors_Center /
            Visitors_Center.pdf

Hours: Grounds
          Daily: 7 a.m.–Dusk

          Visitors Center
          Wednesday–Saturday: 9 a.m.–5 p.m.

Cost: Free

Ages: All ages

Stroller and wheelchair friendly: Yes

Length of visit: 2–4 hours

Description and comments:

Longtime Cincinnati residents might find it ironic to see the word "Fernald" associated with the words "nature preserve." In the 1980's, this uranium processing facility was notorious for releasing uranium dust into the atmosphere, causing radioactive contamination of surrounding areas. Uranium production ceased in 1989 and after several years of an intensive cleanup process, the property has been converted to a nature preserve. Its Visitors Center was Ohio's first LEED platinum-certified green building.

The Visitors Center contains exhibits about the Fernald property and how its use has changed over time since its beginnings as Native American land up through the present time. Before exploring the exhibits, pick up a scavenger hunt page that gives kids a mission and purpose. View Native American artifacts, learn about the early settlers of the land, step into a 1950's living room, and explore life during the Cold War era. See factory memorabilia, view a uranium core replica, and find out about the precautions taken while working in a nuclear facility. Watch a news report explaining the shutdown. Learn about the cleanup process and how a natural habitat was restored in this contaminated area.

After viewing the exhibits, it's time for a hike. Visitors Center personnel will lend you a bag with field guides, binoculars, a magnifying glass, and other tools to help you explore nature. Six different trails of varying lengths and difficulty cover more than seven miles and allow visitors to see five different ecosystems: forest, prairie, savanna, wetlands, and open water. The Shingle Oak Trail is 0.7 miles long and a good choice for kids. Another scavenger hunt sheet is available for this hike. Kids are fascinated by the Bone Yard and are encouraged to observe different plants, trees, rocks, and animals. While the trails remain open until dusk, be sure to return your field bag to the Visitors Center before it closes at 5 p.m.

Fernald Preserve hosts many free events during the year, mostly on weekends. Many of these are ideal for kids. Check the calendar for details.

FORT ANCIENT EARTHWORKS AND NATURE PRESERVE

Address: 6123 State Route 350, Oregonia, OH 45054

Phone: (513) 932-4421
            (800) 283-8904

Website: www.ohiohistory.org / fortancient

Hours: April–November
            Tuesday–Saturday: 10 a.m.–5 p.m.
            Sunday: Noon–5 p.m.

            December–March
            Saturday: 10 a.m.–5 p.m.
            Sunday: Noon–5 p.m.
            Call for scheduled tour starting times.

Cost: $6 Adults
            $4 Children (6–12)
            Free Children 5 and under
            $5 Seniors (60+)
            $8 Park only (no museum admission), per vehicle
            Check for AAA and discounts.

Ages: 8 and up for standard tours
            Group tours for younger children can be
            arranged with advance notice.

Stroller and wheelchair friendly: Yes

Length of visit: 1 hour for museum tour; allow extra time
to explore grounds and hike trails

Description and comments:

Visit Fort Ancient and learn about the prehistory of
Ohio's native people. Archaeological findings range from

when the earliest people hunted mastodons with spears, to when the Adena people became an agricultural society, and then to the time of the European settlers arriving. See tools they developed, such as an atlatl (spear-thrower) and bow and arrow, and items that were traded from as far away as South America. Learn about the earthworks and mounds built by the Hopewell culture, and find out how they were used. See the 18,000 feet of earthen walls surrounding Fort Ancient. The museum contains well-done displays and you can either walk through and read the information yourself or plan your visit around a guided tour. During a tour you may be able to try shooting an atlatl or play a game of double ball, invented by Native Americans. Visit the classroom and open drawers filled with artifacts and other items you can touch. Let your kids bang on the drum. Outside you will discover a Hopewell dwelling, a canoe, and a prehistoric garden. Archaeologists work at Fort Ancient during the summer and if you would like to see them at work on an excavation site, plan to visit in July. The grounds extend beyond the museum area and it is worth your time to see the two scenic overlooks. There are picnic areas, pit toilets, and hiking trails. Fort Ancient has both interesting learning opportunities as well as a beautiful natural setting. Older kids will appreciate the museum, but there are parts that will appeal to younger children as well.

GORMAN HERITAGE FARM

Address: 10052 Reading Road, Evendale, OH 45241

Phone: (513) 563-6663

Website: www.gormanfarm.org

Hours: Monday–Friday: 9 a.m.–5 p.m.
Saturday: 9 a.m.–3 p.m.
Limited winter hours. Check website for details.
Open Sundays in October only: Noon–4 p.m.

Cost: $5 Adults
$3 Children (3–17)
Free Children 2 and under
$3 Seniors (60+)

Ages: All ages

Stroller and wheelchair friendly: Yes
Trails are paved, some have packed gravel.
Call ahead if you need assistance; they will arrange to have you park to avoid the gravel or they will transport you in a golf cart.

Length of visit: 1–4 hours

Description and comments:

Come visit the farm and see and learn about a variety of farm animals. When you arrive, pick up scavenger hunt questions to keep your kids focused and interested. You'll see and learn about chickens, cows, donkeys, horses, pigs, rabbits, sheep, goats, and a turkey. You'll also understand the uses of the farm machinery like combines and tractors while also exploring the buildings on the property. Notice the building with bars on the window made from old wagon wheels. Visit the Children's Garden and see herbs, sunflowers, fruit trees, and a sundial. Learn the reasons to keep a compost pile and what should go into them. If you're lucky, you might catch a glimpse of a hummingbird!

Gorman Heritage Farm sits on 122 acres of land right off of I-75. Visiting the farm allows children to see where their food and farm products originate. They will see freshly laid eggs and wool being sheared from a sheep. Take a hike along a trail (one is stroller/handicap accessible) to see the wildlife in the pond and the trees in the Old Growth Forest.

Gorman has several camps and festivals throughout the year. Check the website for more information.

Wear comfortable shoes, pack sunscreen, a water bottle, and bug spray, and be ready to experience life on the farm in the middle of Cincinnati.

GRANT BOYHOOD HOME AND SCHOOLHOUSE

Address: Grant Boyhood Home:
219 East Grant Avenue, Georgetown, OH 45121

Grant Schoolhouse:
508 South Water Street, Georgetown, OH 45121

Phone: (937) 378-3087

Website: www.ohiohistory.org/granthome

Hours: Memorial Day–Labor Day
Wednesday–Sunday: Noon–5 p.m.

September and October
Saturday and Sunday: Noon–5 p.m.

Cost: One price for both sites:
$3 Adults
$1 Children (6–12)
Free Children 5 and under

Ages: 4 and up

Stroller and wheelchair friendly: No

Length of visit: 1 hour

Description and comments:

Ohio is known as the "Mother of Presidents," and there are several sites of presidential significance near Cincinnati. Two of these are the home and schoolhouse where Ulysses S. Grant spent his early childhood. Start at Grant's Boyhood Home, where you can learn about Grant's upbringing as well as see a typical rural home of the 1800's. Kids will be captivated by the animatronic display of Ulysses at the age of 15 as he discusses his aspirations. You can touch metal objects to activate the display and hear him talk about their significance in his life. There are displays of historical artifacts including the binoculars that Grant used during the Civil War. Walk or drive a few blocks from the boyhood home to the one-room schoolhouse where Grant's formal education began. Both sites are operated under the same management. At the schoolhouse, you will learn how school was conducted with students of all ages in the same classroom. According to our tour guide, this schoolhouse produced four admirals and two generals, in addition to Ulysses S. Grant who was both a general and president.

HANDS AGAINST HUNGER
AT THE HOPE FACTORY

Address: 2430 East Kemper Road, Cincinnati, OH 45241

Phone: (513) 771-2244

Website: www.thechildrenarewaiting.org

Hours: By appointment

Cost: Donations appreciated

Ages: 8 and up to work on assembly line
Younger children may attend with parents

Stroller and wheelchair friendly: Yes

Length of visit: 2–3 hours

Description and comments:

This Adventure is different than any other in this book because it requires you to work. Visitors, even kids, work on an assembly line in a factory. But this isn't an ordinary factory—this is the Hope Factory, where volunteers of all ages come together with donations to produce Hope Boxes™ that contain food, water, and other necessities to feed hungry children all over the world. Hands Against Hunger is a program run by A Child's Hope International, a Christian charity that serves children around the world with programs for adoption, foster care, orphan care, and humanitarian relief.

Register on their website to volunteer for a public session which lasts about two and a half hours. Each session starts with a 30-minute orientation where volunteers learn about malnutrition and the countries which will benefit from the food being packed. You'll have an opportunity to taste the prepared food which contains rice, soy protein, vegetables, and a vitamin powder that reverses malnutrition. Volunteers are then organized into teams. Children ages eight and up work on the assembly line. Younger children can stand with their parents or draw pictures on the boxes in which the food will be shipped. A play area is available, but unsupervised. Trained volunteer supervisors, dubbed the Red Shirt Team, teach volunteers the different tasks on the assembly line. Some volunteers measure ingredients and pour them into a funnel under which another volunteer holds a bag. Another weighs the bag and adds or removes rice until it is the correct weight and another person seals the bag. Volunteers can trade jobs during their shift. Upbeat music is played, creating a fun and festive atmosphere. Most volunteers produce enough food to feed one child for a year during their shift. Together, the volunteers at Hands Against Hunger feed 10,000 children every day.

Working at the Hope Factory gives kids the opportunity to provide meaningful service to others. Kids find the work fulfilling, feel good about helping others, and look forward to returning. Don't be surprised if your child wants to start saving quarters to donate to Hands Against Hunger. Each quarter pays for one meal for a hungry child. Donations are always appreciated, but not required to participate in a packing session. This is an organization about which you can feel good about giving because 90% of money donated goes directly toward feeding hungry children. A Child's Hope International has only two paid employees while the others are volunteers. Most of the equipment and supplies in the Hope Factory have been donated by businesses and individuals. Even the United States Air Force helps by utilizing training missions to deliver Hope Boxes to Haiti from their base at Wright-Patterson, but no funding comes from the government.

HERITAGE VILLAGE MUSEUM
AT SHARON WOODS PARK

Address: 11450 Lebanon Road, Sharonville, OH 45241

Phone: (513) 563-9484

Website: www.heritagevillagecincinnati.org

Hours: May–September
Wednesday–Saturday: 10 a.m.–5 p.m.
Sunday: 1–5 p.m.

Tour Times
Wednesday–Saturday: 10:30 a.m., 12:45 p.m., 3 p.m.
Saturday: 10:30 a.m., 12 p.m., 1:30 p.m., 3 p.m.
Sunday: 1:30 p.m., 3:30 p.m., 3 p.m.

Open other dates throughout the year for special events.

Cost: $5 Adults
$3 Children (5–11)
Free Children 4 and under

Great Parks of Hamilton County
Motor Vehicle Permit:
$3 Daily
$10 Annual

Ages: 3 and up

Stroller and wheelchair friendly: Almost completely

Length of visit: 1–3 hours

Description and comments:
Heritage Village Museum is a collection of about a dozen

historic buildings that depict life as it was in the 19th century. The buildings dating from 1804 to 1891 were rescued from destruction and moved from other locations in the region to recreate a village setting. There are four homes, a summer kitchen, a barn, medical office, mercantile store, print shop, church, one-room schoolhouse, and a train station. During regular operating hours, a tour guide takes you through the buildings. Heritage Village has several special events and programs throughout the year. During special events, there are interpreters in every building with many demonstrations throughout the village. Check the website for dates and prices of special events.

If you plan to attend with a group, call ahead to request that they open the Hands On History Center. Kids ages ten and under love this area where they touch and interact with items that are typically off limits in historic homes. They can recline on an antique bed, pretend to cook at an antique stove, and play with a variety of old-fashioned toys.

HIGHFIELD DISCOVERY GARDEN AT GLENWOOD GARDENS PARK

Address: 10397 Springfield Pike, Cincinnati, OH 45215

Phone: (513) 771-8733

Website: www.greatparks.org/learn/highfield-discovery-garden

Hours: April–October
Tuesday–Saturday: 9:30 a.m.–5 p.m.
Sunday: Noon–5 p.m.

November–March
Wednesday–Saturday: 9:30 a.m.–5 p.m.
Sunday: Noon–5 p.m.

Cost: $5 Adults
$4 Children (2–12)
Free Children under 2,
with accompanying adult

Discounted rates during off season. Family season passes available.

Great Parks of Hamilton County
Motor Vehicle Permit:
$3 Daily
$10 Annual

Ages: 3–8

Stroller and wheelchair friendly: Yes

Length of visit: 2–4 hours

Description and comments:

Within the pastoral Glenwood Gardens park, you'll find

Highfield Discovery Garden. This park is perfect for kids ages 3–8. Younger kids in strollers will also have a great time visiting the park. Kids climb in the 25-foot tall Discovery Tree, designed with kids in mind. Explore inside the trunk, view the park from the branches and hunt for hidden animals within the tree. The Discovery Tree and the whole park are fully accessible for physically challenged visitors. Grandma's Scent Garden was designed for the visually impaired. Many different textures of trees and plants can be felt, and the aroma of the flowers and herbs in this garden will delight everyone. Grandma has a play house complete with table and chairs waiting for a tea party.

The Wizard's Garden includes a boardwalk, a swinging bridge, and a dragon! Fallen trees in the park have been sculpted into some interesting characters. Walk along the hillside and see if you can spot them.

Water the plants in the Vegetable Garden, see the miniature locomotive in the Trolley Garden, smell the flowers in the Butterfly Garden and look for fish, frogs, and dragonflies in Frog and Toad's pond.

Highfield Discovery Garden has educational programs with themes that change every two weeks. See website for details.

These gardens are vibrant, entertaining, and educational, too. While here, don't forget to discover the rest of Glenwood Gardens. A scenic overlook in the park has views of rolling meadows and open woodlands. You will find stroller-friendly paths in the park too. There are no picnic tables available, only some park benches inside of Glenwood Gardens. Bring a large blanket with you and enjoy your picnic on the lawn.

HUESTON WOODS STATE PARK

Address: 6301 Park Office Road, College Corner, OH
            45003

Phone: (513) 523-6347

Website: http://parks.ohiodnr.gov/huestonwoods

Hours: Grounds
            Open daily, year round

            Nature Center
            Daily: 10 a.m.–4:30 p.m.

Cost: Free admission
            Fees charged for some activities

Ages: All ages

Stroller and wheelchair friendly: No

Length of visit: 2 hours–all day

Description and comments:

Hueston Woods State Park offers 3,600 acres with many different recreational opportunities for families. This large park offers camping, cabins, and a lodge for overnight guests, but it also makes a great day trip. Although the park is named after the woods, our favorite part is the lake. Acton Lake is a 625-acre lake that offers a 1,500-foot family-friendly beach, boating, and swimming. There's a bathhouse with restrooms, a concession stand, and even a playground that will keep families happy for hours. Pets are not permitted on the swimming beach, but there is a designated area to the right of the beach for pets. The concession stand even has a doggie menu.

The marina rents canoes, kayaks, pedal boats, motor boats, and pontoon boats. They sell fishing supplies as well as snacks. The Nature Center is also a must-see for families. Indoor exhibits display snakes, turtles, and an aquarium as well as information about the park. Outdoor exhibits allow you to see bobcats, eagles, hawks, owls, and more. Check to see if any naturalist programs are scheduled during your visit. If hiking is your passion, you'll find 12 trails to choose from ranging from easy to moderate. The park contains 200 acres of old-growth forest with beech and sugar maple trees. Fossils are abundant a few places in the park. Ask a naturalist for a map to lead you to the recommended areas. Individuals may keep what they find for their personal collections. Several geocaches are also hidden inside the park. Learn more at www.geocaching.com.

If that isn't enough to keep you busy, you'll find more activities than you'll have time for at Hueston Woods. Explore the park on a bike or horseback. Visit the Pioneer Farm Museum. Play either traditional golf or disc golf. A paintball course and a variety of court sports are also offered.

The park has ten different picnic areas with tables and grills. Dining at the Lodge is another option. The Johnny Appleseed Lounge has a casual dress code and offers sandwiches and pizzas. The Trailblazer Dining Room is open daily for breakfast, lunch, and dinner and has a lovely lake view.

JANE'S SADDLEBAG

Address: 13989 Ryle Road, Union, KY 41091

Phone: (859) 384-6617

Website: www.janessaddlebag.com

Hours: April–October
            Friday: 11 a.m.–8 p.m.
            Saturday and Sunday: 11 a.m.–7 p.m.

Cost: $5 per person admission to petting zoo

Ages: All ages

Stroller and wheelchair friendly: Yes

Length of visit: 2–3 hours

Description and comments:

Jane's Saddlebag is a family owned business operating since 2004. Jane's Saddlebag has a variety of activities on the premises including a petting zoo, a children's village, and a 1700's replica Flatboat.

The petting zoo is the highlight of a trip to Jane's. You'll interact with a variety of animals including a Watusi cow, a pot-bellied pig, a llama, goats, a horse, a donkey, and some very soft and cuddly baby doll sheep. The animals are housed in a barn and are free to roam around in the pasture. A play set with a slide is set up outside of the barn for the goats to show off their climbing skills. Maybe you can encourage the goats to take a trip down the slide!

The children's village is a collection of several small buildings including a chapel, a jail, and a garage. The younger kids especially love to play in these interesting buildings. In front of the village is a large hill that just beckons the children to roll down it. (Grass stain alert! You might want to put the kids in old clothes.)

The 1700's replica flatboat sits at the bottom of this hill and contains educational displays inside. If you need a history refresher, flatboats were the mode of transportation for pioneers as they floated down the Ohio and Mississippi rivers; the boats were eventually disassembled and used to build homes.

Jane's is located on the banks of Big Bone Creek. Sit along the creek and skip stones, dip your feet in the water, or simply watch the boats cruise past you.

A restaurant, gift shop, and wine shop are also found on the grounds of Jane's Saddlebag. They host a number of special events throughout the year. Look for information about these events on their website.

Jane's Saddlebag contains both paved paths and grassy areas. The restaurant, bathrooms, and paved paths are fully handicap-accessible. A large-wheeled stroller is best for the petting zoo and the grassy areas and hills on the premises.

JUNGLE JIM'S INTERNATIONAL MARKET

<u>Address:</u>   5440 Dixie Highway, Fairfield, OH 45014

4450 Eastgate South Drive, Cincinnati, OH 45245

<u>Phone:</u>   (513) 674-6000 Eastgate tours
(513) 674-6023 Fairfield tours

<u>Website:</u>   www.junglejims.com

<u>Hours:</u>   Daily: 8 a.m.–10 p.m.
Tours are scheduled on weekdays only

<u>Cost:</u>   Tours
$5 Adults and children
Jungle Jim's $2 coupon included
with price of tour

<u>Ages:</u>   Store visit: all ages
Tour best for kids 4 and up

<u>Stroller and wheelchair friendly:</u> Yes

<u>Length of visit:</u> Tours last 1 hour
Shopping: allow 1–2 hours minimum

<u>Description and comments:</u>

Jungle Jim's International Market is an amazing grocery store that has been featured on *Food Network, Good Morning America, Time* magazine, *Cincinnati* magazine, and many more. They carry unique and authentic foods, beer, and wines from all over the world. Pulling into the parking lot at the Fairfield location, you'll notice the waterfall, pond, and the life-sized plaster giraffes, elephants, monkeys, and a gorilla all waiting to welcome you to this unique shopping experience. The Eastgate location is hard to miss with a monorail bursting through the front of the building. Both stores are decorated with lots of kid-friendly themes. The displays are unique to each store. While exploring the stores, you might find an animated lion dressed like Elvis singing every five minutes. Some interesting displays include a 1952 fire truck, the Candy Castle, a real Nascar car, a giant dragon, an authentic taxi from India, Pedro the Mariachi Man, and a cereal character band playing 1950's tunes. You'll find an extensive selection of international foods, natural foods, candy, hot sauces, seafood, produce, cheeses, and more. It's fun to challenge your kids to find the most unusual food in the store. On our last visit, we discovered everyone's favorite snack, the dehydrated water bugs. Visit the theater in either location to view the movie explaining the interesting story behind Jungle Jim's stores. A trip to Jungle Jim's isn't complete without a trip to the award-winning bathrooms. From the outside, they appear to be simple portable toilets, but on the inside, they open to nice modern bathrooms.

The tour is an educational addition to your shopping trip. Be sure to arrange this in advance. The tour takes you throughout the store and a guide explains several interesting foods and facts. Learn behind-the-scenes information while tasting many delicious samples. You'll see odd foods like sheep heads and duck feet. Dinner, anyone? Jungle Jim's is truly a unique shopping experience. Allow yourself plenty of time to look around, shop, and explore. We have created a scavenger hunt to use with your kids on your visit, too. Look at our Pinterest page for more information. Have fun shopping!

KINGS ISLAND AND SOAK CITY WATERPARK

Address: 6300 Kings Island Drive, Kings Island, OH 45034

Phone: (513) 754-5700

Website: www.visitkingsisland.com

Hours: Mid-April–Early November
Check website for operating hours and days
Closed to the public most of September

Cost: $32.99 Adults and children 48″ and taller (online price)

$56.99 Adults and children 48″ and taller (regular price)

$30.99 Children 3 and up, under 48″ tall, and ages 62+ (online price)

Free Children 2 and under

Dinosaurs Alive
$5 Adults and Children

Ages: All ages
Must be at least 36″ tall to ride most rides in Planet Snoopy

Stroller and wheelchair friendly: Yes

Length of visit: 2 hours–all day

Description and comments:

Amusement Today readers have voted Kings Island's kids' area as the best in the world. Your children will be thrilled experiencing the rides in Planet Snoopy if they are at least

36 inches tall. This area includes 18 attractions featuring four kid roller coasters. You will never forget the smiles on your kids' faces.

If your kids have graduated from Planet Snoopy, but are not quite ready for The Beast roller coaster, there are many other options in the park for the not-quite-so adventurous. Verify thrill levels and height restrictions for all the rides on the park map. A height of 48″ allows guests the option of experiencing many more rides in the park. See a variety of high quality shows for children and adults. The shows feature singing, and dancing. The dancing fountains at the entrance to the park are also a favorite. Don't forget to ride the elevator up the Eiffel Tower to scan the park from above. Thrill seekers will want to ride the Banshee, the world's longest inverted coaster, added to the park in 2014.

When you need to cool off, take the train to Soak City, the water park at Kings Island. (Only season passholders may use the parking lot entrance.) Smaller kids enjoy their own special area with a zero-depth-entry pool, a mini slide, and a cascading mushroom. There is a raft ride specially designed for a child and a parent. Float on the Splash River not-so-lazy river and ride the waves in either of the two wave pools. There are plenty more exciting rides for bigger kids and parents looking for some adventure. Be sure swimsuits don't have exposed zippers, buckles, rivets, drain holes, or metal ornamentation since these are not allowed on the water slides. Soak City is fun on its own or paired with a day at Kings Island. For the little ones, we recommend choosing one park and spending the day there. Either park could be an entire day's event.

Be aware that visitors are not permitted to bring coolers into the park. You can eat your lunch on the picnic tables outside the main entrance. Another option is to pack lawn chairs in your vehicle and dine in comfort at your car. Concession stands are also located inside the park. Any concession stand will gladly provide cups of ice water so go ahead and leave your water bottle at home.

Dinosaurs Alive! is the world's largest animatronic dinosaur park, with more than 60 life-sized dinosaur models in an outdoor forest setting. This attraction has a separate admission fee. This attraction might be scary for young children.

LAKE ISABELLA

Address: 10174 Loveland-Madeira Road, Loveland, OH
              45140

Phone: (513) 791-1663

Website: www.greatparks.org/parks/lake-isabella

Hours: Grounds
              Daily: Dawn–Dusk

              Fishing Center
              Hours are seasonal; see website

Cost: 12-hour Fishing tickets
              $10 Adults
              $1   Children
              $2.50 Seniors

              Rowboat rental: $10.33 for 6 hours

              Great Parks of Hamilton County
              Motor Vehicle Permit
              $3 Daily
              $10 Annual

Ages: 3 and up

Stroller and wheelchair friendly: Yes

Length of visit: 1–3 hours

Description and comments:

    If you're looking for a one-stop fishing Adventure, this
is it. Lake Isabella is one of the Great Parks of Hamilton
County and has everything you need for a day of fishing.
You don't need to have a state fishing license; just purchase
a daily pass at the park. Kids can fish for 12 hours for just $1.

Make the boathouse your first stop. Purchase your fishing pass and bait. If you don't own fishing equipment, you can rent or buy it here. The onsite store carries a large selection of fishing equipment, plus snacks and drinks. The store personnel can help you figure out the equipment you need and offer some tips for catching fish. The 28-acre lake is stocked weekly from March through October. You can fish from the dock, from shore, or from a boat. Rowboats are available for rental. Although there are some picnic tables located next to the lake, we recommend bringing your own folding chairs.

Enjoy a picnic in one of the shaded picnic areas or eat at the snack bar at the boathouse. If your kids need a break from fishing, take them to the playground. Our kids thought this playground was especially fun. The park also has access to the scenic Little Miami River. During summer months, Lake Isabella hosts Friday Night Grillouts. You can purchase food and beverages and enjoy live music.

LEBANON MASON MONROE RAILROAD

Address: Lebanon Station:
             127 South Mechanic Street, Lebanon, OH 45036

             Mason Station:
             5660 Tylersville Road, Mason, OH 45040

Phone: (513) 933-8022

Website: www.lebanonrr.com

Hours: Operates most weekends during spring,
             summer, and fall, and some Wednesdays and
             Fridays during the summer. Also operates
             during Christmas season. Check website for
             operating schedule.

Cost: One hour train ride:
             $13 Adults
             $8 Children (5–16)
             $5 Children (2–4)
             Free Children 1 and under
             $8 Seniors

             Weekend themed events are priced separately.
             Check website for details.

             LM&M recommends purchasing
             all tickets in advance.

Ages: All ages

Stroller and wheelchair friendly: No, but foldaway
wheelchairs and strollers can be stowed.

Length of visit: 1–2 hours

Description and comments:

Enjoy the scenic beauty of the Warren County countryside from aboard a vintage train. Lebanon Mason Monroe (LM&M) Railroad operates one-hour train rides, during which you can learn about railroad history and operation, or simply enjoy the ride from either your passenger coach or the open-air gondola. Railroad conductors have a wealth of knowledge to share. Many family-friendly events are scheduled on weekends throughout the year, with themes such as Curious George, Thomas the Tank Engine, and Pumpkin Patch Express.

The trains are not currently heated or air-conditioned, so dress appropriately. There are restrooms at the train station, but not on the train. Plan to arrive 20 minutes in advance of the scheduled departure time in order to park, pick up tickets, and use the restroom. Boarding begins 15 minutes prior to the departure time. Make sure you have cash if you would like to purchase food on the train.

LITTLE MIAMI BIKE TRAIL

Address: Milford to Urbana, along the Little Miami River

Website: www.miamivalleytrails.org/little-miami-scenic-trail

Hours: Open daily, year round, during daylight hours

Cost: Free

Ages: All ages

Stroller and wheelchair friendly: Yes

Length of visit: 2–4 hours

Description and comments:

This paved bike trail follows the picturesque Little Miami River, a federal and state scenic river. Charming stores and unique refreshment stands can be found along the trail. Walk, bike, rollerblade, ride your horse, or even cross country ski on the 75-mile trail. The trail intersects with roads and inactive railroad crossings, so you will want to pay close attention to your smaller riders to keep them safe. Bike rental locations dot the trail along the way. Check the website for a map of the trail, bike rental information, and lists of restaurants at stops along the way.

Some other notable stops along the trail include Camp Dennison (milepost 1.3) which was a Volunteer Recruiting Service for training of Union troops before the Civil War. Fort Ancient (page 119) is at milepost 26.6 and the Birthplace of Tecumseh (milepost 53.7) is where this great Shawnee leader had his beginnings.

LOVELAND CASTLE - CHATEAU LAROCHE

Address: 12025 Shore Road, Loveland, OH 45140

Phone: (513) 683-4686

Website: www.lovelandcastle.com

Hours: April–September
          Daily: 11 a.m.–5 p.m.

          October–March (Weather Permitting)
          Saturday and Sunday: 11 a.m.–5 p.m.

Cost: $3 per person

Ages: 2 and up

Stroller and wheelchair friendly: No

Length of visit: 1–2 hours

Description and comments:

One of Cincinnati's most unique attractions, the Loveland Castle, or Chateau LaRoche, was the dream of one man, Harry Andrews, and his Boy Scout troop (named the Knights of the Golden Trail). It was built to resemble a medieval European Castle. Taking advantage of its location on the Little Miami River, Andrews used rocks from the river and bricks he made himself to construct the castle. The Knights of the Golden Trail organization is still in existence and its primary activity is operating the castle. On your visit, you learn more about the castle construction and its features. Watch the video about Harry Andrews and his time building the castle. Look for the rocks in the wall that have come from places all over the world. Investigate the design of the front door, and then inquire about how it could keep out intruders. Descend to the basement and check out the dungeon. Plan to spend time exploring the beautiful gardens. Don't forget your camera! Take advantage of a great backdrop for some photographs of the kids. Next, wander down to the river. This is a great spot for a picnic lunch. Note that there are two portable restrooms, but no indoor restrooms. Also, the circular stairs in the castle are steep and narrow and will make the parent of a young toddler nervous. Preschoolers and school-age children will have fun exploring the castle.

MARIEMONT BELL TOWER CARILLON

Address: Pleasant Street, Mariemont, OH 45227

Phone: Contact Richard Gegner for tours
             (513) 271-8519

Website: www.mariemont.com

Hours: Tours by appointment only

Cost: Free

Ages: 5 and up

Stroller and wheelchair friendly: No

Length of visit: 1 hour (allow extra time to play at the park)

Description and comments:

Tucked away along Route 50 in the charming and historic town of Mariemont is Dogwood Park. Within Dogwood Park is a wonderful surprise, the Bell Tower Carillon. A carillon is a musical instrument that contains at least 23 large bells. The Bell Tower Carillon in Mariemont is 100 feet high and contains 49 bells covering four different octaves. Call about a week in advance and schedule a tour of this amazing landmark.

To begin this tour you will ride an old and small elevator to the room where the carillon is played. You might need to board the elevator in shifts of 3–4 people. The carillon is small and holds a maximum of 6–8 people at once. The carillonneur will explain the history of the tower and play a song to demonstrate how the notes are played. You'll be amazed at the amount of strength and talent it takes to play a melody. Next, climb about 12 steps up to view the bells in the tower. Examine the two-ton bell "Bourdon" and all the other bells that make up this musical instrument. Your tour guide will stay downstairs and will play some of the different bells so you can watch, feel, and hear the vibrations and sound of these large bells. The Bell Tower Carillon has recently undergone major renovations; the facilities are updated and a little roomier than before.

Concerts are held every Sunday and on holidays. Hear the concert at 7 p.m. during the summer and at 4 p.m. during the winter. On holidays the carillon plays at 2 p.m. The first Sunday in August is always a special concert for kids. Bring some lawn chairs or a blanket and enjoy.

Be sure to pack a lunch and take advantage of the picnic tables at Dogwood Park. The Tot Lot entertains with two playsets. The mature trees comfortably shade the park, keeping it cool on hot summer days. Dogwood Park also has nature trails to explore.

MEGALAND AT COLERAIN PARK

Address: 4725 Springdale Road, Cincinnati, OH 45251

Phone: (513) 385-7503

Website: www.colerain.org/department/public-
services/township-parks/colerain-park/

Hours: Daily: Daylight hours

Cost: Free

Ages: 2–10

Stroller and wheelchair friendly: Yes

Length of visit: 1–2 hours

Description and comments:

   Megaland is a large, community-built playground inside
Colerain Park. This is a special, out-of-the-ordinary park. It
is a wooden playground with lots of places to climb, slide,
and play. Zip lines, multi-level climbing structures, curvy
slides, and more keep kids busy for hours. It has many
features that are different from the average playground.
It is a great place to visit with kids who have lots of extra
energy. The park also has picnic tables, shelters, and a one-
mile walking trail.

METAMORA, INDIANA

Address: Metamora, IN 47030

Phone: (765) 647-6512

Website: www.metamoraindiana.com

Hours: Gristmill
           April–mid-December
           Wednesday–Sunday: 9 a.m.–5 p.m.

           Canal boat rides
           May–October
           Wednesday–Sunday: hourly, Noon–4 p.m.

Cost: Canal boat rides
           $5 Adults
           $2 Children (4–12)
           Free Children 3 and under
           $4 Seniors (60+)

Ages: 3 and up

Stroller and wheelchair friendly: Yes

Length of visit: 2–4 hours

Description and comments:

   Visiting Metamora, Indiana, takes you a step back in time.
Metamora is an 1838 canal town that contains Indiana's
oldest operating water-powered grist mill. Visit the mill
and examine the method used to separate the wheat or corn
into differing grain sizes. You can purchase their freshly
ground products and take them home and bake some fresh
cornbread. Be sure to refrigerate or freeze your cornmeal. It
has a short shelf life without preservatives.

The canal boat ride is the other feature the kids will remember. The boat ride, powered by horses, transports passengers along the canal and over the aqueduct. The purpose of the aqueduct is to carry canal water over an existing waterway. This is the only remaining covered bridge aqueduct in the United States and is an American Civil Engineering Landmark. Your captain will explain the history of how the canals were built, how Indiana paid for them, and how they were made obsolete by the railroads. See the graffiti on the inside of the aqueduct, some of which has been there for many years. After the ride, your kids will have a chance to visit and pet the horses.

Feed the ducks along the river and then dine at one of the many restaurants for lunch. Candy, fudge, and ice cream stores will keep the kids happy, too. You will find an abundance of gift and antique stores in Metamora; just be careful if you take little ones into these shops. Many are located in historic buildings and have tight spaces and breakable merchandise on low shelves. The stores are open according to their own schedules. Check the website for a list of stores and their operating hours.

If you're interested in other activities, a 2.6-mile hiking and biking trail stretches along the canal. Check the website for information on carriage rides and horseback riding in the area. Between shopping, eating, seeing the gristmill, and taking a canal boat ride, you will have a full day ahead of you in Metamora.

New attractions in Metamora include the Metamora Museum of Oddities and the Metamora Gem Mine. See the website for more information.

MIAMI WHITEWATER FOREST

Address: 9001 Mt. Hope Road, Harrison, OH 45030

Phone: (513) 367-4774

Website: www.greatparks.org/parks/miami-
            whitewater-forest

Hours: Grounds
            Daily: Dawn to Dusk

            Visitor Center
            Hours are seasonal; see website

Cost: Activity fees apply for boat and bike rentals,
            camping, golf, and Parky's Pirate Cove

            Great Parks of Hamilton County
            Motor Vehicle Permit:
            $3 Daily
            $10 Annual

Ages: All ages

Stroller and wheelchair friendly: Yes

Length of visit: 2–4 hours

Description and comments:

Miami Whitewater Forest is the largest of the Great
Parks of Hamilton County. It sits on 4,343 scenic acres about
30 minutes northwest of Cincinnati on the western side of
Hamilton County.

The Visitor Center encourages kids to learn about
the nature of the park by meeting an animatronic James
Audubon. Mr. Audubon explains the features and the history
of the park, provides some of his personal background as

an artist, a painter, and a naturalist, and encourages kids to talk to the naturalists throughout the park. A life-sized beaver lodge is fun for kids to explore. Inside the lodge a video of beavers building the lodge and taking care of babies is shown. Be sure to find the room within the Visitor Center with live animals, too. On hand are turtles, snakes, salamanders, and toads. You'll also see some fuzzy animals like a bunny and a tarantula! Free crafts are also available in this room. Upstairs look for books, puzzles, and nature-based computer games. Learn all about the birds in the park by studying bird sounds, nests, and habitats. See the website for Visitor Center hours.

The park contains two paved trails including the 1.4-mile Parcours fitness trail equipped with stations along the trail encouraging physical exercises like pull-ups, sit-ups, and other strength and endurance activities. There are also several unpaved nature trails and two horseback riding trails.

Boats and bicycles are available for rent in the boathouse. The four-person quadracycle is especially fun for families. Campsites, fishing areas, soccer fields, and a 9-hole disc golf course are also available within the park. New in 2014 is the largest dog park in the region, the 11-acre Simmonds Family Dog Park.

The 18-hole golf course is a favorite spot for those who like to take to the links. For families trying out the course, take note that junior fees are charged for children 17 and younger during specific hours.

Parky's Pirate Cove is the super fun wet playground located within Miami Whitewater Forest. See the separate listing for this attraction on page 158. A snack bar and traditional playground are also available.

OZO PLAY CAFÉ

<u>Address:</u>   10004 Montgomery Road, Cincinnati, OH
             45242

<u>Phone:</u>   (513) 834-9459

<u>Website:</u>   www.ozoplaycafe.com

<u>Hours:</u>   April–September
             Monday–Friday: 9 a.m.–1 p.m.
             Saturday: 9:30 a.m.–1 p.m.

             October–March
             Monday–Thursday: 9 a.m.–3 p.m.
             Friday–Saturday: 9 a.m.–1 p.m.

<u>Cost:</u> $7 for the first child
             $4 per additional child
             Monthly unlimited plans also available

<u>Ages:</u>   6 and under

<u>Stroller and wheelchair friendly:</u> Yes

<u>Length of visit:</u> 1–3 hours

<u>Description and comments:</u>

   Sometimes it's difficult finding the perfect place to take your little ones to play. OZO Play Café is a cozy, clean, and creative spot young children are sure to enjoy. Parents will appreciate the comfortable seating areas where they can relax and chat with friends while sipping a cup of coffee. It's small enough to be able to keep an eye on your kids anywhere in the building and big enough for them to play, explore, and create. This is an ideal place to meet a friend to share some adult conversation while the little ones are busily playing.

Kids six and under are welcome to play at OZO Play Café. Unique ride-on toys, a playset with a slide, chalkboards, play kitchens, crayons, easels, and squishy balls create endless opportunities for make-believe play. The toys found at OZO are designed to encourage creativity. Young kids love to play in this special space created just for them. An area in the back is set aside just for babies. It is outfitted with play mats, books, stacking toys, and bouncy balls to keep the littlest ones entertained.

OZO carries a small selection of drinks and snacks including coffee and tea, juices, graham crackers, cookies, and fruit snacks. They do not carry a full lunch menu, so plan on having a meal before or after playing. Pack along some socks for everyone. Both kids and adults are asked to remove their shoes before playing. Parents are asked to wear socks, but kids can choose to either wear socks or go barefoot. If you find that your child can't live without some of the unique toys offered here, OZO has a retail area with toys available for purchase. Although OZO is specifically for kids 6 and under, if older kids are with you, there is no charge for them to come in, enjoy a snack, read a book, or engage in any other quiet activity while the younger kids play.

PARKY'S FARM AT WINTON WOODS

Address: 10073 Daly Road, Cincinnati, OH 45231

Phone: (513) 521-3276

Website: www.greatparks.org/learn/parkys-farm

Hours: Open daily
           Pony Rides, Wagon Rides and PlayBarn are
           available during select times:

           Spring and Fall
           Friday: 10 a.m.–4 p.m.
           Saturday: 11 a.m.–6 p.m.
           Sunday: Noon–6 p.m.

           Summer
           Monday–Friday: 10 a.m.–5 p.m.
           Saturday: 11 a.m.–6 p.m.
           Sunday: Noon–6 p.m.

Cost: $3 Pony Rides
           $2.50 Parky's PlayBarn
           $2.50 Wagon Rides

           Great Parks of Hamilton County
           Motor Vehicle Permit:
           $3 Daily
           $10 Annual

Ages: All ages
           PlayBarn: 2–12
           Must be 48″ or shorter to ride ponies

Stroller and wheelchair friendly: Yes

Length of visit: 2–4 hours

Description and comments:

Parky's Farm is great fun for young children. Part of Winton Woods Park, Parky's Farm is a 100-acre demonstration farm with orchards, gardens, and live animals including goats, pigs, sheep, and chickens. Stroll around the farm to look at the animals. If a staff member is available, kids might be able to get up close to the animals. Kids love the PlayBarn, an old dairy barn that was converted into a two-story indoor playground with a farm theme. Outside the PlayBarn you'll find kid-sized, pedal-operated John Deere wagons that kids can drive around.

Parky's Farm also has pony rides and wagon rides for an additional fee. Picnic areas and an outdoor playground are also available. On most Fridays from May through October, Parky's has Fantastic Farm Fridays with additional activities that vary with the season. In the spring, kids might be able to try milking a goat or watch a sheep being sheared. In the fall, they might visit a pumpkin patch. Parky's Farm hosts several special events each year. Sign up for the free e-mail newsletter from the Great Parks of Hamilton County to receive information about special events.

PARKY'S WET PLAYGROUNDS

Address: Parky's Ark at Winton Woods
            10245 Winton Road, Cincinnati, OH 45231

            Parky's Pirate Cove at Miami Whitewater Forest
            9001 Mt. Hope Road, Harrison, OH 45030

            Parky's Wetland Adventure at Woodland Mound
            8250 Old Kellogg Road, Cincinnati, OH 45255

Phone: (513) 521-7275

Website: www.greatparks.org/activities/playgrounds

Hours: Memorial Day through Labor Day
            Daily: 11 a.m.–7 p.m.

Cost: $2.50 Children (2–12)
            $6 for 3 children
            Free Adults and children 1 and under

            Great Parks of Hamilton County
            Motor Vehicle Permit:
            $3 Daily
            $10 Annual

Ages: 1–7

Stroller and wheelchair friendly: Yes

Length of visit: 1–3 hours

Description and comments:

    Wet playgrounds are located within three different
Great Parks of Hamilton County. Each different playground
is uniquely decorated with various animals and trees
spraying and squirting water. Small slides, giant turtles, and
tipping coconuts are all part of the fun! There is no standing

water, so it's safe for the little ones. A separate area is fenced to keep visitors ages three and under safe. You and your children should wear swimsuits because everyone will be sure to get wet. Babies and toddlers need to wear swim diapers. Kids will go crazy playing in the dancing fountains and the cascading mushroom waterfalls. Pack your lunch (picnic facilities are available in the park) or buy a treat from the snack bar. There are plenty of restroom facilities and changing areas. Bring your sunscreen and prepare to wear the kids out.

PYRAMID HILL SCULPTURE PARK & MUSEUM

Address: 1763 Hamilton-Cleves Road, State Route 128, Hamilton, OH 45013

Phone: (513) 868-1234

Website: www.pyramidhill.org

Hours: Park Hours
Daily: 8 a.m.–5 p.m.

Museum Hours
Daily: Noon–5 p.m.

Cost: $8 Adults
$3 Children (6–12)
Free Children 5 and under

Ages: All ages

Stroller and wheelchair friendly: Some trails are accessible, but most sculptures can be viewed from vehicle. Restrooms are accessible.

Length of visit: 1–2 hours

Description and comments:

Pyramid Hill combines the beauty of nature with sculptural art. This is an attraction that we suggest you visit with an open mind. You will find a wide array of huge sculptures made from steel, granite, bronze, aluminum, polychrome, wood and more. Some are natural, some painted, and some polished. All are interesting and unique. Walk right up to the sculptures, touch them, and even walk through them. Children may not be interested in the sculptures or they may love them. The park is situated on

355 acres overlooking the Great Miami River with both paved roads and hiking trails throughout. The park also offers gardens, lakes, and picnic facilities. Special programs for children are conducted during the summer; check the website for details.

Also on the grounds is the Ancient Sculpture Museum which displays Egyptian, Greek, Roman, and Etruscan sculptures. The museum contains over 70 pieces of artwork and is best for children ages 10 and up. Inside the museum is a Roman style courtyard and garden.

RABBIT HASH, KENTUCKY

Address: 11646 Lower River Road, Union, KY 41091

Phone: (859) 586-7744 (General Store)

Website: www.rabbithashusa.com

Hours: Store hours:
          Daily: 10 a.m.–7 p.m.

Cost: Free to visit

Ages: All ages

Stroller and wheelchair friendly: Yes

Length of visit: 1–3 hours

Description and comments:

What is the only listing in *Adventures Around Cincinnati* claiming a dog as the mayor? Well, it's Rabbit Hash, Kentucky, of course! Rabbit Hash can be found on the National Register of Historic Places. It is a quirky little town along the Ohio River right across from Rising Sun, Indiana. It's about a 30-minute drive from downtown Cincinnati.

Rabbit Hash was established in 1813 and is one of a few early 19th century towns still in existence. It was in 1998 when the first dog was elected mayor and the tradition still continues today. The mayor is generally available to shake hands, meet visitors, and pose for photos. The Rabbit Hash General Store is known as the best preserved country store in Kentucky. Stop in and discover the unique merchandise found inside. This store carries an eclectic variety of products including homemade soaps, candles, lotions, floral-decorated cowboy boots, baskets, candy, antiques, cough medicine, and a list of other products too numerous to mention. Ask for a cold sarsaparilla or grape Nehi soda and enjoy your beverage as you sit on the front porch of the store or stroll along the banks of the river.

If you are hungry for dinner, The Scalded Hog is a barbeque restaurant in Rabbit Hash. It is open only on the weekends.

The town has several buildings full of antique products for sale including wrought iron beds, bird houses, watering cans, tools, signs, and much more. Along the road, you'll find two antique gas pumps adding to the charm of the town. Play on the banks of the river, watch the motorcycles drive in, and enjoy the unique charm of this small hamlet.

RUMPKE LANDFILL TOUR

Address: 3800 Struble Road, Cincinnati, OH 45251

Phone: (513) 741-2617

Website: www.rumpke.com/education/facility-tours

Hours: By appointment, on Wednesdays only

Cost: Free

Ages: Tour participants must be at least 4

Stroller and wheelchair friendly: No; tour buses are not equipped with wheelchair lifts. Groups may also supply their own handicap accessible tour bus.

Length of visit: 45-minute tour

Description and comments:

Did you know that there is an elephant buried in the Rumpke Landfill? Or that the world's biggest chocolate bar is also buried deep inside this landfill? Learn about these and many more interesting facts and stories about the Rumpke Landfill during their 45-minute tour. This is an educational tour for kids and adults. It's an out-of-the-ordinary tour for anyone who would like to learn more about what happens to their trash after it leaves their garbage cans. Rumpke provides a tour bus and a knowledgeable tour guide to take your group through the facility. Tours are scheduled for ten or more people, but if you have a smaller group, they will try to add you to another tour.

During your 45-minute visit, you remain on the bus the entire time. The tour guide describes many facts about Rumpke including the history of the company, the design of the landfill, and methods for removing methane gas from the decomposing trash. As you pass through the facility, witness the large machinery crushing the waste into tiny pieces and even smell the clean air thanks to the deodorizers keeping the scents of the trash to a minimum. The tour guide emphasizes the importance of recycling and keeping recyclable waste out of the landfill. This is a great Adventure for a field trip or for kids who are fascinated with big trucks and trash collection.

Check their website for availability of tours of their other facilities including the recycling centers. Recycling tour participants must be high school age and up.

SHARON WOODS

Address: 11450 Lebanon Road, Sharonville, OH 45241

Phone: (513) 563-4513

Website: www.greatparks.org/parks/sharon-woods

Hours: Grounds
             Daily: Dawn to Dusk

             Sharon Centre and Boathouse
             Hours are seasonal; see website

Cost: Adventure Station
             $2.50 Children (2–12)
             Free Parents accompanying children

             Activity fees apply for boat and bike rentals,
             and golf

             Great Parks of Hamilton County
             Motor Vehicle Permit:
             $3 Daily
             $10 Annual

Ages: All ages
             Adventure Station: 2–10

Stroller and wheelchair friendly: Yes

Length of visit: 2–4 hours

Description and comments:

   Among the Great Parks of Hamilton County, Sharon
Woods is a favorite for families because of the many different
recreational opportunities. Sharon Centre serves as a visitor
center for the park and the gateway to Heritage Village
Museum (see page 127). Outside Sharon Centre are picnic

tables and a traditional playground. Inside you'll find a gift shop, a small Nature Center, and the Adventure Station which is an indoor playground. The Nature Center has free educational exhibits including a computer quiz game and some live animals such as salamanders, turtles, and a snake.

The Adventure Station is a perfect place to let your kids burn some energy when the weather prevents them from playing outside. Most of the Adventure Station has a nature theme. Kids climb up stairs through the inside of a tree, and then play in the tree house above. They crawl through tunnels to a giant bird's nest. Also on the upper level you will find themed rooms. Kids pretend they are in jail, climb into a covered wagon, and sit on a saddle. If you lose track of your kids, you won't have to climb a tree to find them. Look for a set of stairs in one of the corners. An attendant sits guard at the bottom to prevent little ones escaping without their parents. Ask the attendant about the scavenger hunt. There is a Children's Corner reserved for 2–5 year olds with a ball pit and small slide.

At the other end of this 730-acre park is Sharon Lake and Harbor. The Boathouse rents rowboats, pedal boats, mini-pontoon boats, kayaks, canoes, motorboats, and bicycles. Boating is a lively activity for teens. Fishing is permitted from the boats or a fishing pier. The harbor area also has a playground for kids. Although this isn't a full-size wet playground, there are a few water features, so pack some swimsuits and sunscreen when the weather is warm. The harbor area offers a snack bar, picnic areas, and access to a paved trail around the lake and a Parcours fitness trail. Avid hikers won't want to miss the striking scenery along the 0.7-mile Gorge Nature Trail. Sharon Woods also offers an 18-hole golf course with a pro shop, snack bar, and clinics and discounts for Junior Golfers ages 7–17.

TRAMMEL FOSSIL PARK

Address: Tramway Drive, Sharonville, OH 45241

Website: www.sharonville.org/188/Trammel-Fossil-Park

Hours: Daylight hours

Cost: Free

Ages: 3 and up

Stroller and wheelchair friendly: No

Length of visit: 1–2 hours

Description and comments:

Trammel Fossil Park is located in the midst of an industrial park in Sharonville. This 10-acre piece of property has avoided development. Here you can investigate the exposed earth and hunt for fossils. No special tools are required; most of the fossils are loose rocks that you will find right below your feet. There are signs explaining the theories of what happened on this land throughout history. Climb to the top and take in a bird's eye view looking south towards Cincinnati. Be sure to wear sturdy shoes for climbing on the hillside. Kids who are interested in fossils will love this place! Please note that there are portable toilets available during the summer months, but no running water on the premises. You are permitted to bring a representative sample of fossils home with you.

TRI-STATE WARBIRD MUSEUM

Address: 4021 Borman Drive, Batavia, OH 45103

Phone: (513) 735-4500

Website: www.tri-statewarbirdmuseum.org

Hours: Wednesday: 4 p.m.–7 p.m.
            Saturday: 10 a.m.–3 p.m.

Cost: $12 Adults
          $7 Students
          $7 Veterans
          Free to veterans in uniform and WWII veterans

Ages: 8 and up

Stroller and wheelchair friendly: Yes

Length of visit: 1–2 hours

Description and comments:

This 20,000-square-foot facility houses over ten aircraft. Six of these aircraft are operational. The Warbird Museum stresses the importance of preserving the stories of a world at war and of honoring the people who have served our country. A display of historical artifacts relates to the history of the museum's aircraft.

When you arrive, ask to see the film explaining the history of these airplanes. The museum also has a replica of WWII barracks and other items commemorating the efforts made by soldiers in this war.

The aircraft are stored in a hangar where planes are being restored. See the beautifully painted warbirds together in one place. These restored and operational planes—including the *Cincinnati Miss* and *Tweety*—are occasionally flown by their owners. Be careful with small kids because tripping hazards may exist on the hangar floor. Check the website for more information on the planes in their collection and pictures and video of the planes in action.

American History field trips are available to junior or senior high school students. Admission costs are waived for field trips and the cost of transportation will also be reimbursed. See website for more details.

WARREN COUNTY HISTORY CENTER AND GLENDOWER

Address: Warren County History Center:
           105 South Broadway / Ohio Route 48, Lebanon,
           OH 45036

           Glendower Mansion:
           105 Cincinnati Avenue, Lebanon, OH 45036

Phone: (513) 932-1817

Website: www.wchsmuseum.org

Hours: Museum
           Tuesday–Friday: 10 a.m.–4 p.m.
           Saturday: 10 a.m.–5 p.m.
           Closed holidays

           Glendower Mansion
           Seasonal. See website for details.

Cost: Museum only
           $5 Adults
           $3.50 Children (5–18)
           $4.50 Seniors (65+)
           $15 for a family with up to four children

           Museum and Glendower Mansion
           $8 Adults
           $5 Children (5–18)
           $7 Seniors (65+)
           $28 for a family with up to four children

Ages: 4 and up

Stroller and wheelchair friendly: Museum only

Length of visit: 1–2 hours

Description and comments:

The Warren County History Center's main exhibit area, Harmon Hall, houses a vast collection of items dating from prehistoric days to the early 1900's. The museum is expertly detailed and interesting for both parents and kids. A few favorite displays are the pioneer era collection of farming equipment, tools, and other items the pioneers used, including a sausage stuffer. On the main floor of the museum is the Village Green. This display is worthy of a much larger museum. The floor is lined with small storefronts featuring a toy store, drug store, post office, and many more. Inside each store front are many everyday objects from the early days of life in Warren County and Southern Ohio. Have your kids try to imagine what life would have been like without cell phones, computers, and TVs.

Other treasures inside this museum are The Butterworth Cabin, which was once an Underground Railroad stop and an old country school complete with McGuffey readers. A large display on transportation shows carriages, sleighs, and even a 1908 Buick.

Glendower Mansion, located just a few blocks from the museum, offers tours with costumed interpreters. Glendower is a Northern Antebellum Greek Revival period home. It is shown as it would have been from 1845–1865. The home is located on five pristine acres with grounds suitable for tossing your blanket down and enjoying a picnic. Inside the home you'll see the period furnishings along with the history of the county. Glendower is not wheelchair or stroller accessible. See website for operating schedule.

WINTON WOODS

Address: 10245 Winton Road, Cincinnati, OH 45231

Phone: (513) 521-7275

Website: www.greatparks.org / parks / winton-woods

Hours: Grounds
Daily: Dawn to Dusk

Boathouse
Hours are seasonal; see website

Cost: Activity fees apply for boat and bike rentals,
riding center, and golf

Winton Queen Tour Boat
$4 Adults
$3 Children and Seniors

Great Parks of Hamilton County
Motor Vehicle Permit:
$3 Daily
$10 Annual

Ages: All ages

Stroller and wheelchair friendly: Yes

Length of visit: 2–4 hours

Description and comments:

Winton Woods is one of the most visited of the Great
Parks of Hamilton County. The highlight of this 2,555-acre
park is the Harbor area. Many types of boats and bicycles
are available for rental at the boathouse. The *Winton Queen*
tour boat is a full-size pontoon boat and takes visitors on
weekend tours of the lake. Find Parky's Ark wet playground

in the Harbor area; see listing on page 158. Also find a traditional playground, snack bar, and amphitheater.

The Winton Woods Riding Center is a horseback riding facility available for riders of all levels. They have 35 horses, two outdoor arenas, an indoor riding hall, an open field and a hunter course, and a 2.6-mile horse trail. Lessons, trail rides, camps, and a Special Rider's Program for disabled riders are offered.

Golfers can choose from two separate golf courses at Winton Woods. Meadow Links is a 9-hole course and Mill Course is an 18-hole course. Golfing options here include lessons, leagues for adults and kids, camps, lessons, and tournaments. Check the website for free clinics offered.

Parky's Farm is a 100-acre educational farm with live animals, wagon and pony rides, an indoor Parky's Playbarn, and more. See separate listing on page 156 for more information.

The Parcours Trail is a fitness trail equipped with stations along the trail encouraging physical exercises like pull-ups, sit-ups, and other strength and endurance activities. Quite popular for walking, jogging, biking, and rollerblading is the paved 2.6-mile trail around the lake. The Great Oaks nature trail is .7 miles one-way and the Kingfisher nature trail is 1.1 miles one-way. Strollers and wheelchairs can be used on the paved trail, but are not recommended for the nature trails.

Winton Woods has what disc golf enthusiasts consider to be one of the best disc golf courses in the area. It is one of only two 18-hole courses in the park district. This course sees quite a bit of use so be prepared for crowds.

WOLF CREEK HABITAT

Address: 14099 Wolf Creek Road, Brookville, IN 47012

Phone: (513) 312-9143

Website: www.wolfcreekhabitat.org

Hours: October–April
Saturday and Sunday: 11 a.m.–5 p.m.
Interactions end at 4 p.m.

May–September
Saturday: 10 a.m.–6 p.m.
Interactions end at 5 p.m.
Sunday: 10 a.m.–5 p.m.
Interactions end at 4 p.m.

Cost: Donations appreciated to cover food
Wolf viewing: free
Wolf Interactions: $20 donation per person

Ages: Wolf Viewing: all ages
Wolf Interactions: by staff discretion

Stroller and wheelchair friendly: No

Length of visit: 1–2 hours

Description and comments:

Southern Indiana might be an unexpected place to find a wolf education and rescue facility, so Cincinnatians are very fortunate to have a facility like this so close to home. Observing the wolves is a treat, but interacting with them is a memory you're not likely to forget.

Wolf Creek Habitat was established in 2000 by Terry and Kathy Baudendistel. At the time of publication, it is home to 32 wolves. A raised platform provides an excellent view of the wolves so you can see them from above. The staff might give visitors marshmallows to toss to the wolves in order to entice them to come out of their dens. Who knew wolves had a sweet tooth? Wolf viewing is available every weekend, but be aware that the wolves are most active when the temperature is cooler.

After you've had a chance to view the wolves, decide if you're ready for a closer encounter. Weekend wolf interactions are not scheduled in advance; just let a staff member know you're interested. There is no set age requirement for this activity; staff members will determine if children are able to remain calm and follow instructions before allowing them to enter the enclosure. While Wolf Creek Habitat is unable to guarantee anyone's safety around these wild animals, in all of their years of operation, no visitor has ever been bitten.

Interacting with the wolves is an amazing experience. Expect to receive some "wolfy kisses" and for the wolves to rub up against you. When the wolves are shedding their winter coats, they may allow you to help pull off some fur. For the interactions, wear clothing that you don't mind getting dirty: long pants, close-toed shoes, and nothing with fringe or anything the wolves could grab. It is best not to wear hair in a ponytail because the wolves might mistake it for a toy and tug it. Small cameras are permitted in the enclosure.

Private wolf interactions can also be scheduled on Fridays for a $30 donation per person, but these are frequently booked up months in advance. Before you leave, browse the unique items in the gift shop. All purchases help support the care and feeding of the wolves.

WOODLAND MOUND

Address: 8250 Old Kellogg Road, Cincinnati, OH 45255

Phone: (513) 474-0580

Website: www.greatparks.org/parks/woodland-mound

Hours: Grounds
Daily: Dawn to Dusk

Seasongood Nature Center
Hours are seasonal; see website

Cost: Activity fees apply for golf and Parky's Wetland Adventures

Great Parks of Hamilton County
Motor Vehicle Permit:
$3 Daily
$10 Annual

Ages: All ages

Stroller and wheelchair friendly: Yes

Length of visit: 2–4 hours

Description and comments:

Woodland Mound sits on a 1,000-acre piece of property above the Ohio River in Anderson Township. In addition to a stunning vista of the river, Woodland Mound has much to offer. Seasongood Nature Center serves as a welcome center for the park and is staffed by a naturalist and volunteers. Explore exhibits on the main floor, loft, and lower level. A life-size replica of a sycamore tree has doors for kids to open to discover the types of animals living in the trees. Look up and see if you can spot other types of animals, too.

Interactive displays teach about animals and plants. Learn to distinguish between butterflies and moths, insects and insect relatives, nocturnal and daytime animals, and edible and inedible plants. Several exhibits are displayed at the perfect height for little tots. Look into a chipmunk den, match trees with leaves, and build an animal. The upper loft area contains books, games, and puppets, as well as an outdoor observation deck. The lower level includes a nature touch table with pine cones, feathers, bark, and more. Live animals on display at Seasongood include a toad, tarantula, turtle, and snake.

A popular feature of Woodland Mound is the 18-hole disc golf course located opposite the Nature Center. In addition to gifts and books, the gift shop (inside Seasongood) sells flying discs for the course. Next to Seasongood Nature Center is Breezy Point Pavilion where you'll find Parky's Wetland Adventure (see page 158), a snack bar, and a playground. There are also several trails to choose from: a 0.9-mile Parcours fitness trail equipped with stations along the trail encouraging physical exercises like pull-ups, sit-ups, and other strength and endurance activities; two nature trails; and a 1.2-mile paved trail. There are also many picnic areas, a campground, and an 18-hole golf course that offers classes, lessons, and camps for Junior Golfers ages 7–17. A family could easily spend hours and hours at Woodland Mound taking in all of the experiences.

WORLD'S LARGEST HORSESHOE CRAB

Address: 664 West Main Street (Route 28), Blanchester,
           OH 45107

Phone: (937) 625-4091

Website: www.freedomworshipbaptist.com/crabpage

Hours: Daylight hours

Cost: Free

Ages: All ages

Stroller and wheelchair friendly: Yes

Length of visit: <1 hour

Description and comments:

Quirky roadside attractions, especially the "world's largest" kind, are just plain fun and appreciated by kids and adults alike. Many families enjoy seeking these out while traveling, but might not know that we have one here in Greater Cincinnati. The World's Largest Horseshoe Crab is located at Freedom Worship Baptist Church in Blanchester. As with most roadside attractions, it can be viewed at any time and requires no admission fee. The crab measures 24 feet wide and 12 feet tall. It is hollow, allowing visitors to walk underneath it.

Horseshoe crabs have been around for a long time and their earliest fossils are found in strata from the Ordovician period. This crab was originally created for the Baltimore Columbus Center Maritime Museum in Maryland. It was obtained by the Creation Museum and donated to Freedom Worship Church in 2006. In 2008, a motorcyclist jumped over the crab. The World's Largest Horseshoe Crab has a tie to the movie *Eclipse,* of the *Twilight Saga.* In the movie, the main character Bella is presented with a quilt that her mother crafted from the souvenir T-shirts purchased during their travels. One of the quilt squares depicts the crab.

While the World's Largest Horseshoe Crab is definitely the main attraction, the church grounds also offer gardens to explore. The Scripture Garden surrounds the crab and features plants found in the Bible. Calvary's Hill & Garden Tomb features a representation of Jesus' empty tomb.

DAYTON

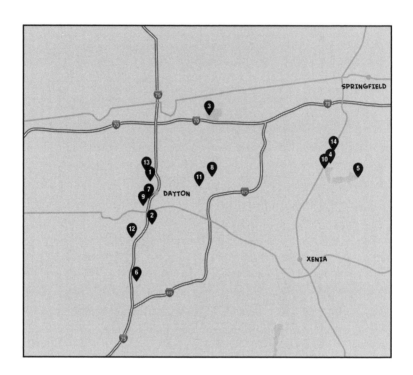

1   Boonshoft Museum of Discovery

2   Carillon Historical Park

3   Carriage Hill MetroPark

4   Clifton Gorge State Nature Preserve

5   Clifton Mill

6   Cox Arboretum MetroPark

7   The Dayton Art Institute

8   Dayton Aviation Heritage National Historic Park -
    Huffman Prairie Flying Field Interpretive Center

9   Dayton Aviation Heritage National Historic Park - Wright Cycle Company Complex

10 Glen Helen Nature Preserve and Raptor Center

11 National Museum of the United States Air Force

12 SunWatch Indian Village/Archaeological Park

13 Wegerzyn Gardens MetroPark

14 Young's Jersey Dairy

BOONSHOFT MUSEUM OF DISCOVERY

Address: 2600 DeWeese Parkway, Dayton, OH 45414

Phone: (937) 275-7431

Website: www.boonshoftmuseum.org

Hours: Monday–Saturday: 9 a.m.–5 p.m.
          Sunday: Noon–5 p.m.
          Closed some holidays

Cost: $12 Adults
          $9 Children (3–16)
          Free Children 2 and under
          $10 Seniors (60+)
          50% Discount with Cincinnati Museum Center
          or Cincinnati Zoo Membership

Ages: All ages

Stroller and wheelchair friendly: Yes

Length of visit: 2 hours–all day

Description and comments:

Boonshoft Museum of Discovery has a little bit of everything for kids of all ages. Younger children enjoy That Kids Playce, where they can dig in a pit of rubber shavings for dinosaur "bones," build with blocks, climb up the Tree House and slide back down. There are replicas of a SunWatch Thatched Hut, Pioneer Cabin, and Paul Lawrence Dunbar House. The Baby Garden is designed especially for children under 2. Older children love the three-story Climbing Tower and Slide. In Oscar Boonshoft Science Central, kids learn principles of science firsthand playing with an air blower, water table, and construction area. Kids can watch cool science experiments in the Science Theater and conduct experiments themselves in the Do Lab. Visit the planetarium (included with admission price) for amazing full-color films with 3D options and brilliant images of the stars.

On the second floor, visitors discover more about wildlife and natural history. At the Tidal Pool, reach down and touch starfish, sea anemones, and sea cucumbers. One of our favorite places is the Discovery Zoo, with over one hundred animals and insects, completely indoors. Children and adults are enthralled with the playful river otters. Kids learn through pretend play in themed areas such as a landfill and recycling center, woodlands, an animal hospital, a courthouse, and a garage. Older children should investigate the exhibits on the Sonoran Desert, Glowing Geology, and the African Room. Amateur bird watchers love to wander out to the Tree House filled with interactive displays.

Make sure you pick up a daily schedule when you arrive so that you can plan your day around the shows and activities that interest you. There is a snack area with vending machines, but no restaurant. With such a diverse set of exhibits, there is surely something that will fascinate every member of your family. It is definitely worth the drive to Dayton.

CARILLON HISTORICAL PARK

Address: 1000 Carillon Boulevard, Dayton, OH 45409

Phone: (937) 293-2841

Website: www.daytonhistory.org

Hours: Monday–Saturday: 9:30 a.m.–5 p.m.
Sunday: Noon–5 p.m.
Closed some holidays

Cost: $8 Adults
$5 Children (3–17)
Free Children 2 and under
$7 Seniors

Check for AAA Discount

Ages: 3 and up

Stroller and wheelchair friendly: Yes

Length of visit: 3–6 hours

Description and comments:

Carillon Historical Park celebrates Dayton's rich history of invention. Set up like a village, it consists of over 30 historical structures with various exhibits. The park is named for the 151-foot-tall Deeds Carillon. A carillon is a bell tower consisting of at least 23 bells. Deeds Carillon has 57 bells and is Ohio's largest. Concerts are performed every Sunday at 3 p.m. from May to October.

The most significant exhibit is the original 1905 *Wright Flyer III*, the world's first practical airplane, which is also a National Historic Landmark. On October 5, 1905, Wilbur flew 24 miles in 39 minutes 23 seconds, longer than the total duration of all the flights of 1903 and 1904. Other Wright

Brothers exhibits include a replica of the Wright Brothers' Cycle Shop and family artifacts.

Other inventions displayed in the park include the cash register and automobile self-starter. Transportation exhibits show the evolution of transportation with displays of a Conestoga wagon, bicycles, early automobiles, an original lock of the Miami and Erie Canal, a trolley car, and locomotives. The park is also a great place to learn about the lifestyles of early Dayton residents. You can tour historic homes, a gristmill, a covered bridge, early gas station, print shop, tavern, and a one-room schoolhouse.

Within Carillon Historical Park is the Heritage Center which is included with general admission. It features exhibits highlighting the entrepreneurial spirit, manufacturing accomplishments, and innovation in Dayton. Within the Heritage Center find a multi-sensory 4-D theater and the Carousel of Dayton Innovation. This is a full scale, Ohio-made carousel featuring hand-carved and hand-painted figures from Dayton's history. Some of the unique figures include an NCR cash register, a Huffy bicycle, a Soap Box Derby Car, and a Mike-Sell's potato chip bag. Ride tokens are available to purchase for $1 per ride.

The Carillon Brewing Company will soon be a part of Carillon Historical Park. It will have costumed interpreters explaining 19th century brewing methods and techniques. They will have daily demonstrations and multiple exhibits featuring the brewing history of Dayton. A beer garden and restaurant will also be on site. This exhibit is free to enter and does not require admission to Carillon Historical Park.

The park includes a café where you can have lunch. Carillon Historical Park provides a great opportunity to see a lot of history in one location.

CARRIAGE HILL METROPARK

Address: 7800 E. Shull Road, Dayton, OH 45424

Phone: (937) 278-2609

Website: www.metroparks.org/Parks/CarriageHill/
Home.aspx

Hours: April–October
Tuesday–Saturday: 10 a.m.–5 p.m.

November–March
Tuesday–Sunday: Noon–4 p.m.
Closed some holidays

Cost: Free

Ages: All ages

Stroller and wheelchair friendly: Gravel or grass paths,
large-wheeled strollers are best

Length of visit: 1–4 hours

Description and comments:

Immerse yourself in 1880's farm life at Carriage Hill
Farm. The farm setting includes reconstructed and historical
buildings including a blacksmith shop, woodshop, historic
house, and barn. Park workers dress in period clothes and
present historical talks and demonstrations from 10 a.m.–
Noon and 1–4 p.m. each day. Demonstrations might include
churning butter, cooking, or horses pulling plows. Kids like
the demonstrations and petting the farm animals. Visiting
Carriage Hill gives you the feeling that you are actually
living on a farm in 1880. On the third Saturday of each month
from 8:30–9:15 a.m., Carriage Hill has a program in which
participants can help the farmer with chores like feeding the

animals and collecting eggs. Preregistration is required for this program. A visitor's center contains additional exhibits on the history of the area and a children's interactive center. There are several hiking and bridle trails for exploring the beautiful park grounds that include woodland and meadow areas, a fishing lake, and marsh. One short hike takes you to an old cemetery. There is an old-fashioned country store that sells candy by the piece. Be sure to stop there for an inexpensive treat for the kids. Picnic tables are available right outside the store. Consider packing your lunch if you visit on a weekday since the snack bar is not always open.

CLIFTON GORGE STATE NATURE PRESERVE

Address: 2331 State Route 343, Yellow Springs, OH 45387

Phone: (614) 265-6453

Website: www.ohiodnr.com/location/dnap/clifton/
tabid/882/Default.aspx

Hours: Daylight hours

Cost: Free

Ages: 3 and up

Stroller and wheelchair friendly: No

Length of visit: 1–3 hours

Description and comments:

Just west of Clifton Mill sits Clifton Gorge State Nature Preserve. This park has been called one of the nation's 50 Most Beautiful Places by *National Geographic*. This picturesque park has trails along the Little Miami River. This river had the honor of being named a National Scenic River in 1973. Many different trails are available to choose from, most overlooking the river far below in the deep gorge. Be careful to watch your kids near the steep cliffs and wear good walking shoes. The Narrows Trail is a perfect place to begin. It's a one-mile trail with some breathtaking views of the park. Many overlooks allow you to marvel at the beauty of the gorge. One interesting overlook explains the story of Darnell's Leap. The legend explains that Darnell was a member of Daniel Boone's team who was captured by Indians. He escaped into the woods but was pursued by his captors. At the narrow part of the gorge, Darnell miraculously leaped across the gorge and avoided being recaptured.

Follow the map and watch the signs while walking the trails. Gaze at waterfalls and maybe spot some wildlife. Your hike could range from one to six miles round trip. The Narrows Trail is fairly level terrain with no steep climbs. Other trails are longer and more challenging. The trails are not paved and are not stroller friendly. Be sure to bring your camera because you will want to remember the beauty of this hike.

CLIFTON MILL

Address: 75 Water Street, Clifton, OH 45316

Phone: (937) 767-5501

Website: www.cliftonmill.com

Hours: See website for restaurant hours
            Closed some holidays

Cost: Restaurant meals range from $3.99 to $8.99

            Tour (Available Sundays)
            $3 Adults and Children

            Christmas Lights
            Day after Thanksgiving–January 1
            $10 Adults and children 7 and up
            Free Children 6 and under
            Free Parking

Ages: 5 and up

Stroller and wheelchair friendly: Yes

Length of visit: Tour lasts about 30–45 minutes

Description and comments:

Clifton Mill is one of the largest water-powered grist mills still in existence. It remains as the only survivor of seven mills originally in the area. A visit to this mill will let you experience a slice of Ohio history. Tour the first floor and see the inner workings of the mill. Touch the giant grindstones and hear the water rushing under your feet providing the power for the mill. The miller describes the basic procedure for grinding wheat and corn and explains the history of the mill and the town. You will learn how life was different in this area before the Industrial Revolution.

The walls of the mill are decorated with over 300 antique flour bags. Some of these bright and colorful bags are over 100 years old and were used as advertising for mills across the country.

On the grounds is a 90-foot authentic wooden covered bridge that crosses the Little Miami River. From the bridge you have attractive views of the Mill, Clifton Gorge, and the river and its waterfalls. Don't forget your camera! Next door is a 1940's gas station with memorabilia, old signs, and original products.

Christmas at Clifton Mill is spectacular, too! The entire area including the mill and waterfall are decorated with 4 million lights. Yes, you read that right, 4 million lights. Be there at 6 p.m. when the lights are turned on and see the area illuminated. They spend three months putting up the lights for a stunning show. See a collection of Santas, a huge outdoor miniature village, and a synchronized light and music show. This is worth the drive!

Within walking distance of the Mill are the Clifton Opera House, The Clifton Historical Society Museum, The Fish Decoy Company, and Weber's Antique Mall. Make sure you also walk to Clifton Gorge State Nature Preserve (see previous listing).

Check the Clifton Mill website for a diagram, pictures, and explanations of how the mill works.

COX ARBORETUM METROPARK

Address: 6733 Springboro Pike, Dayton, OH 45449

Phone: (937) 434-9005

Website: www.metroparks.org/parks/coxarboretum

Hours: April–October
Daily: 8 a.m.–10 p.m.

November–March
Daily: 8 a.m.–8 p.m.
Closed Christmas and New Year's Day

Cost: Free

Ages: All ages

Stroller and wheelchair friendly: Yes

Length of visit: 2–4 hours

Description and comments:

Cox Arboretum is a 189-acre park overflowing with walking paths, trees, gardens, prairies, and more. The park contains one mile of paved paths and 2 ½ miles of unpaved trails (unpaved trails are not stroller or wheelchair friendly). While exploring the park, you will discover many unique features including the Tree Tower. This 46-foot tower is the newest addition to Cox Arboretum. This observation tower provides fantastic views of the trees below and panoramic vistas. The tower is only accessible by steps, so it is not handicap or stroller friendly.

Another unique feature of Cox Arboretum is the Butterfly House. This Butterfly House is open in July and August and has free admission. It contains only native southwest Ohio butterflies and moths in all stages of development. Check their website for a list of ten things to do while visiting the Butterfly House.

Kids love to explore the Children's Maze which is made up of 1,175 boxwood bushes creating a path to the center of the maze. Parents can watch the children explore the maze from an overlook nearby.

Other features in the park include an edible garden, water garden, rock garden, a conifer collection, a wildflower collection, and a Clematis arbor surrounded by 40 varieties of crab apple trees. Cox Arboretum MetroPark is a beautiful park with lots of unexpected surprises to keep kids of all ages entertained.

Many educational programs are offered at Cox Arboretum. Café Sci offers science education once a month and the Eureka! Lab is a three-hour drop-in program that encourages kids to learn and problem-solve. Check their website for a complete list of educational programs and tours. The website also contains scavenger hunts to use in the park, a Scouts Guide, and a Garden Manners Guide.

THE DAYTON ART INSTITUTE

Address: 456 Belmonte Park North, Dayton, OH 45405

Phone: (937) 223-5277

Website: www.daytonartinstitute.org

Hours: Tuesday–Friday: 11 a.m.–8 p.m.
             Saturday: 10 a.m.–5 p.m.
             Sunday: Noon–5 p.m.
             Closed some holidays

Cost: $8 Adults (suggested donation)
             Free Children (17 and under)
             $5 Seniors (60+) (suggested donation)
             Some special exhibitions may have different fee

Ages: 3 and up

Stroller and wheelchair friendly: Yes

Length of visit: 1–5 hours

Description and comments:

   The Dayton Art Institute is a great place to introduce your kids to fine art. It has an area just for kids called the Experiencenter, located in the lower rotunda, which is open the same hours as the rest of the museum. It contains two rotating exhibitions so there is something new every six months. These exhibitions always include real art, displayed at kids' eye level safely behind clear plastic, paired with hands-on educational activities. Their goal is for kids to look at the art and then complete the activity. They try to have something for all ages to enjoy, since visitors include toddlers as well as grandparents, but most activities are geared for the 8 to 12-year-old crowd. It might be challenging for kids to enjoy the galleries after the Experiencenter, so we recommend starting in the galleries and when the kids start getting restless, move on to the Experiencenter.

The museum gallery collections include ancient art, Native American art, glass, textiles, and various other pieces from all parts of the world. As we were touring, we had our children choose their favorite piece in each room and tell us why they liked it. This engaged them in the art and compelled them to think about it, and, as a result, they explored the galleries for far longer than we anticipated. The art institute also offers Gallery Hunts which consist of a checklist of items to find. These are available at the front desk or in the Experiencenter. Another popular program is the Kids Club, which is free, but requires registration. Your child will receive a Gallery Hunt and once they have completed four gallery hunts, they will receive a free art kit.

DAYTON AVIATION HERITAGE NATIONAL HISTORICAL PARK

Address: Wright Cycle Company Complex
16 S. Williams Street, Dayton, OH 45402

Huffman Prairie Flying Field Interpretive Center
2380 Memorial Road, Wright-Patterson Air
Force Base, Dayton, OH 45433

Phone: Wright Cycle Company Complex
(937) 225-7705

Huffman Prairie Flying Field Interpretive Center
(937) 425-0008

Website: www.nps.gov/daav

Hours: Wright Cycle Company Complex
Daily: 8:30 a.m.–5 p.m.
Closed some holidays

Huffman Prairie Flying Field Interpretive Center
Daily: 8:30 a.m.–5 p.m.
Memorial Day to Labor Day: 8:30 a.m.–6 p.m.
Closed some holidays

Cost: Free

Ages: 4 and up

Stroller and wheelchair friendly: Yes

Length of visit: 2–4 hours

Description and comments:

Dayton is the "Birthplace of Aviation," and this national park provides a fantastic opportunity for your kids to learn about the Wright brothers and their quest to build a flying machine. The Wright Cycle Company Complex includes the Wright Cycle Company building, the Wright-Dunbar Interpretive Center, and the Aviation Trail Visitor Center and Museum. At the Wright-Dunbar Interpretive Center, learn about Wilbur and Orville Wright, as well as Paul Laurence Dunbar, an internationally-acclaimed African-American writer. Watch a film about the Wright brothers and explore interactive exhibits about their early careers in printing and bicycles, and their trials and errors in the process of inventing the airplane. Be sure to visit the Wright brothers' print shop and one of their bicycle shops, located adjacent to the interpretive center.

The Huffman Prairie Flying Field Interpretive Center is located near the field where the brothers performed their flying experiments. This center tells the continuing story of the Wright Brothers after their success at Kitty Hawk and has exhibits about the advancement of aviation. A favorite exhibit is the flight simulator where you take a turn maneuvering the *Wright Flyer III.* The film about the Wright brothers is also shown in this center.

Both interpretive centers offer a Junior Ranger program. Ask for the free booklet that contains activities for your child to complete. Upon completion, they present it to a ranger, receive a certificate and pin, and are sworn in as a Junior Ranger. Each site has different activities in the booklet and a different pin, so your child can receive pins from both locations.

Please note that your GPS unit may not correctly direct you to this park. Make sure to print out directions before you leave.

GLEN HELEN NATURE PRESERVE AND RAPTOR CENTER

Address: 405 Corry Street, Yellow Springs, OH 45387

Phone: (937) 769-1902

Website: www.glenhelen.org

Hours: Grounds
            Daily: Dawn–Dusk

            Visitor Center
            Monday–Friday: 9:30 a.m.–4:30 p.m.
            Saturday and Sunday: 10 a.m.–4 p.m.

            Raptor Center
            Winter: 9 a.m.–5 p.m.
            Spring & Fall: 9 a.m.–6 p.m.
            Summer: 9 a.m.–7 p.m.

Cost: $2 Parking
            Donations appreciated

Ages: 4 and up

Stroller and wheelchair friendly: No

Length of visit: 2–4 hours

Description and comments:

Among the many fascinating features of the nature preserve at Glen Helen is the spring that inspired the town's name: Yellow Springs. Kids are quick to point out that the spring is actually orange, not yellow! Antioch College is the home of Glen Helen. An alumnus of the college donated the wooded glen in memory of his daughter, Helen. Additional gifts of land expanded the preserve to include

1000 acres with 20 miles of trails. Today the property is used for educational purposes, both for the college's classes and for the community.

Start your day at the Visitor Center. The 50-cent trail map is an excellent investment. It points out places of interest and provides a short description of each. Before heading off to the trails, check to see if the Trailside Museum is open. Staffed primarily by volunteers, it has irregular hours and features exhibits with hands-on displays ideal for children. Also note the rules that are listed on the map. Collecting, swimming, and wading are all prohibited. Some of the trails are located adjacent to cliffs, so be sure to discuss safety with kids before setting off.

Points of interest on the trail include Pompey's Pillar, a large rock column; The Cascades, a waterfall with a bridge above it; a Hopewell Indian Mound; The Grotto, a small waterfall coming off a reddish travertine mound; and an old dam. Involve your children in choosing which sights to see and plot your route. One must-see sight is the Raptor Center, a facility which rehabilitates injured hawks, owls, and other birds of prey. Visitors can see several of the birds on display. You can either hike or drive to the Raptor Center which is located one mile from the visitor center. If you choose to hike, be aware that there are no public restrooms at the Raptor Center.

The Nature Shop is located in the same building as the Visitor Center and offers nature-oriented merchandise that supports the operation of Glen Helen. Many guided hikes and other programs are offered; check their website for a calendar. The Glen Helen Outdoor Education Center offers day and overnight camps for kids ages 5–15 in the summer as well as residential programs for 4th–6th graders during the school year.

NATIONAL MUSEUM OF THE UNITED STATES AIR FORCE

Address: 1100 Spaatz Street, Dayton, OH 45433

Phone: (937) 255-3286
            (937) 253-4629 (for movie information)

Website: www.nationalmuseum.af.mil

Hours: Daily: 9 a.m.–5 p.m.
            Closed some holidays

Cost: Free parking and admission to museum

            Digital 3D Theatre
            See website for prices

Ages: 3 and up

Stroller and wheelchair friendly: Yes

Length of visit: 2–4 hours

Description and comments:

The Air Force Museum is a must-see for anyone who is even mildly interested in aviation and the history of aviation. There is so much to see and learn that you will easily enjoy this amazing museum. Wear your walking shoes to see over 17 acres of exhibits. Your visit begins with the Wright Brothers and early attempts at aviation, continuing chronologically through to the stealth fighters.

This is the world's largest and oldest military aviation museum. It contains over 360 aircraft and aerospace vehicles, thousands of historical items, and many interactive exhibits. You'll learn about the history of flight and how it became the precision technology of today.

You will be in awe of the massive size of some of these aircraft. Crane your neck to take in the towering Intercontinental Ballistic Missiles. Walk through four Presidential aircraft including the Boeing 707 which carried the body of President Kennedy. You will understand the role of aviation in the defense of our country.

The museum contains a Digital 3D Theatre and three interactive simulators. The Space Shuttle Landing Simulator is free of charge. There is a separate charge for two of the simulators. Museum tours are offered weekdays at 1:30 p.m. and Saturdays at 10:30 a.m. On Fridays at 12:15 p.m. is a Behind the Scenes tour of the restoration hangers. Participants must be over 12 years old and registration is required for this tour. Check the website for more information. A souvenir shop, book store, and cafeteria are also available.

Each month, the museum hosts a Family Day from 10 a.m. to 3 p.m. Each Family Day has a different theme and offers hands-on activities and demonstrations. All of the activities are free. Check the website for the schedule and themes.

SUNWATCH INDIAN VILLAGE / ARCHAEOLOGICAL PARK

Address: 2301 W. River Road, Dayton, OH 45418

Phone: (937) 268-8199

Website: www.sunwatch.org

Hours: Tuesday–Saturday: 9 a.m.–5 p.m.
            Sunday: Noon–5 p.m.
            Closed some holidays

Cost: $6 Adults
            $4 Children (6–16)
            Free Children 5 and under
            $4 Seniors (60+)

Ages: 3 and up

Stroller and wheelchair friendly: Yes

Length of visit: 2 hours

Description and comments:

   SunWatch Village is a National Historic Landmark and the original site of an 800-year-old Native American village. Begin your visit inside with a film explaining more about the village and its history. The interpretive center also holds exhibits to explain the lifestyle of the Fort Ancient Native American culture. Learn about the food they grew in their garden and how they stored it. See how their houses were set up. Next, venture outside to experience life in the village. Excavations took place from 1971 to 1988 and revealed a planned settlement. SunWatch has now partly reconstructed the village. Walk the circle path and see homes, meeting places, and other structures. The buildings feature realistic props like animal skins on the small beds and vegetables ready to be cooked over the fire. Many signs around the park explain the purposes of each structure and everyone is encouraged to ask questions. Kids will have a better understanding of prehistoric Native American culture after their visit to SunWatch.

WEGERZYN GARDENS METROPARK

Address: 1301 E. Siebenthaler Avenue, Dayton, OH
            45414

Phone: (937) 277-6545

Website: www.metroparks.org/Parks/WegerzynGarden

Hours: Park Grounds
            April–October
            Daily: 8 a.m.–10 p.m.
            November–March
            Daily: 8 a.m.–8 p.m.

            Closed Christmas and New Year's Day

            Children's Discovery Garden
            June–August
            Daily: 10 a.m.–8 p.m.
            April, May, September, October
            Daily: 10 a.m.–6 p.m.
            November–March
            Daily: 10 a.m.–4 p.m.

Cost: Free

Ages: All ages
            Children's Discovery Garden is designed for
            ages 3–11.

Stroller and wheelchair friendly: Yes

Length of visit: 2–4 hours

Description and comments:

Wegerzyn Gardens is a delightful gem in Dayton worth discovering. Start your visit at the Children's Discovery

Garden, where kids learn and play at the same time. The garden mimics the different habitat areas found in Ohio including woods, prairie, wetlands, and a cave. Each of these areas has interactive features for kids. They can dig, build a fairy house, look for fossils in a cave, and peek at roots through a root window. They can also pump water into a watering can and water the plants in the garden. Other features include a sand play table, music maze, and playhouse. Be sure to pack a swimsuit, sunscreen, and towel, so your kids can shower themselves under the waterfall.

On weekdays from Memorial Day through Labor Day, Wegerzyn offers a special kids' activity at 2 p.m. that lasts 30–45 minutes. It is different each day and could include feeding the fish, story time, games, or an adventure walk.

Spend some time exploring the rest of the park. Stroll through beautiful formal gardens and follow the boardwalk trail through a swamp garden. There is also a nature trail for those who want to hike. Pack a lunch to enjoy at the picnic facilities.

YOUNG'S JERSEY DAIRY

Address: 6880 Springfield-Xenia Road, Yellow Springs, OH 45387

Phone: (937) 325-0629

Website: www.youngsdairy.com

Hours: Call or check website for seasonal hours

Petting Zoo
April–October: 10 a.m.–10 p.m.
November–March: 10 a.m.–6 p.m.

Cost: 25 cents for goat food
$2 Moovers and Shakers train ride
$1 Giant slide ride
$5.50–$14 Bucket of golf balls
$1.50–$6 Putt-putt golf

Ages: All ages

Stroller and wheelchair friendly: Yes

Length of visit: 4–5 hours

Description and comments:

Young's Jersey Dairy has a plethora of activities to entertain you on your visit. Bring some change to purchase feed for the animals in the petting zoo. It will set you back 25 cents for a handful of specially formulated goat feed with grains, vitamins, and minerals to keep the goats healthy. Kids are thrilled to have the goats nibble the feed right from their hands. The cows and pigs are there, too, but not for feeding. Ride the Moovers and Shakers train which runs during the summer and takes your kids on a trip around the farm. You'll keep everyone busy on the giant slide, two different miniature golf courses, a driving range, and batting cages.

Be sure to plan your trip to include a meal. Choose from two different restaurants. The Golden Jersey Inn has some great food available in a charming barn made with wooden pegs and wood plank siding. The kids' menu includes traditional favorites and also their yummy homemade chicken and dumplings. The grown-up menu also includes traditional favorites, a lighter section, salads, soups, and sandwiches, many with a unique spin. They are also vegetarian friendly. Make sure to save room for dessert, as Young's is famous for its ice cream desserts. The kids' meals include a scoop of ice cream, but you can request a coupon to redeem later at The Dairy Store, the other onsite restaurant. Check the website for complete menus and prices.

Young's hosts many special events on weekends throughout the summer and fall. The corn maze is open to visitors beginning in August and starting in September Young's popular wagon rides take you on a ride to the field to pick your own pumpkin. Check the website for details. If you're interested in extending your day, John Bryan State Park is just a few miles away, as is the Little Miami Bike trail. Many Young's guests do their bicycling then reward themselves by indulging in a creamy treat!

A HOP, SKIP,
AND A JUMP

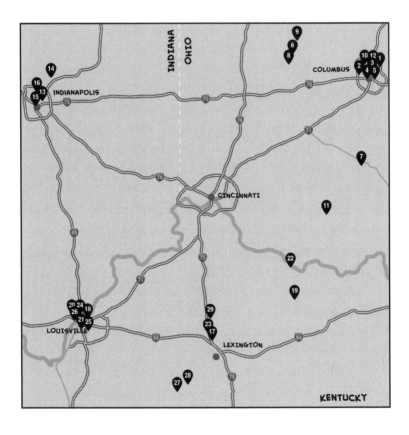

These Adventures are more than an hour from Cincinnati, but less than two hours.

OHIO

1   American Girl® Boutique and Bistro
2   Anthony-Thomas Chocolate Factory
3   Central Ohio Fire Museum & Learning Center
4   COSI
5   Franklin Park Conservatory and Botanical Gardens
6   Freshwater Farms of Ohio
7   Hopewell Culture National Historic Park
8   Johnny Appleseed Educational Center & Museum
9   Ohio Caverns
10 Ohio Statehouse
11 Serpent Mound
12 The Topiary Park

INDIANA

13 Children's Museum of Indianapolis, The
14 Conner Prairie Interactive History Park
15 NCAA Hall of Champions
16 The Virginia B. Fairbanks Art & Nature Park: 100 Acres

KENTUCKY

17 American Saddlebred Museum
18 Belle of Louisville
19 Evergreen Hills Maze
20 Frazier History Museum
21 Kentucky Derby Museum
22 Kentucky Gateway Museum Center
23 Kentucky Horse Park
24 Kentucky Science Center
25 Louisville MEGA Cavern
26 Louisville Slugger Museum & Factory
27 Old Fort Harrod State Park
28 Shaker Village of Pleasant Hill
29 Toyota Visitor Center and Plant Tour

OHIO

AMERICAN GIRL® BOUTIQUE AND BISTRO

Address: 4040 The Strand East, Columbus, OH 43219

Phone: (877) 247-5223

Website: www.americangirl.com/stores/location_col.php

Hours: Store
Monday–Thursday: 10 a.m.–8 p.m.
Friday–Saturday: 10 a.m.–9 p.m.
Sunday: 11 a.m.–6 p.m.

Bistro Dining Room
Monday–Thursday: 10 a.m. –5:30 p.m.
Friday–Saturday: 10 a.m.–7:30 p.m.
Sunday: 11 a.m.–4:30 p.m.

Cost: Bistro
Appetizers: $4–7
Entrees: $8–15
Desserts: $4–7
Afternoon Tea and Craft: $12 per person

Doll Hair Salon
Hair styles: $10–25
Ear piercing: $14

Ages: 4–12

Stroller and wheelchair friendly: Yes

Length of visit: 2–4 hours

Description and comments:

Since 1999, some lucky girls have enjoyed pilgrimages to the American Girl® Place in Chicago. We are happy that the opening of an American Girl® Boutique and Bistro in

Columbus puts this special treat within both physical and financial reach of more families. It's still a splurge, but now it no longer requires an expensive hotel stay in downtown Chicago. The drive to Columbus and back is an easy day trip for families in Cincinnati.

In addition to shopping, American Girl® Columbus offers a restaurant and a doll salon. The American Girl® Bistro is a special dining experience designed specifically for the delight of little girls. Doll chairs are provided so that girls and dolls can dine side by side. If you don't have a doll or forgot to bring one, they will loan you one for the duration of your meal. Waitresses dote on the girls and also provide tea cups and saucers for the dolls. The menu is small but has kid-friendly food and some choices for the adults as well. Choose from appetizers, entrees, and desserts, or on weekdays opt for afternoon tea.

The Doll Hair Salon is not only fun, but is a great way to spiff up the hair of an older doll. First, the doll is strapped into a salon chair and a cape is tied on. Girls can choose from a menu of hairstyles, and then watch as the doll's hair is transformed. The stylists engage the girls in conversation during the process. Other services offered include ear piercing and a doll facial scrub.

It is best to plan this Adventure well in advance. Bistro reservations can be made months in advance, while Doll Hair Salon reservations are made on the same day. For maximum efficiency, it is best to arrive about 15 minutes prior to your dining reservation in order to make the salon appointment. Allow 75 to 90 minutes for your meal prior to your salon appointment so that you aren't rushed. Because American Girl® is located in Easton Town Center, a large shopping center, the men and boys in your family can easily find other restaurants and activities.

American Girl® has a large retail store with dolls, clothing, accessories, and books. Check the website to see if any special events or crafts are scheduled for the day of your visit. If you are not familiar with American Girl® merchandise, look over the website before you go. To ensure a positive experience and minimize disappointment, we recommend discussing your spending allowance in advance.

ANTHONY-THOMAS CHOCOLATE FACTORY

<u>Address:</u>   1777 Arlingate Lane, Columbus, OH 43228

<u>Phone:</u>   (614) 274-8405
             (877) 226-3921

<u>Website:</u>   www.anthony-thomas.com

<u>Hours:</u>   Tuesday & Thursday: 9 a.m.–3 p.m. for tours
             (no reservation necessary)

             Monday–Thursday: 9 a.m.–3 p.m. for groups
             of 10 or more by appointment only

<u>Cost:</u> $2 Adults (19+)
             $1 Children (3–8)
             Free Children 1 and under

             Admission fee is returned as a gift certificate
             toward purchase

<u>Ages:</u>   3 and up

<u>Stroller and wheelchair friendly:</u> Yes

<u>Length of visit:</u> 1 hour (allow extra time to shop
in the gift shop)

<u>Description and comments:</u>

   If you love chocolate be sure to visit Anthony-
Thomas Chocolate Factory. Take part in a guided tour
of the chocolate factory from a catwalk overlooking the
production floor. The Anthony-Thomas factory makes over
25,000 pounds of chocolates each shift. Gaze at the huge
copper kettles and the silver wrapped pipes containing
liquid chocolate. The tour guide explains each step of the
chocolate making process from harvesting the beans to the

packaging of delicious candy. At the end of the tour enjoy a complimentary buckeye candy or a crème-filled chocolate. Help your children understand that these treats originate somewhere other than the grocery store. We were told that the employees are allowed to have as much chocolate as they want to eat. We didn't see anyone taste any, but maybe you will!

The weeks leading up to Easter are a great time for a tour. Chocolate production goes into high gear with people working around the clock making chocolate bunnies, crème-filled eggs, and other Easter treats. Tens of thousands of chocolate bunnies are made each year. They range in size from three inches tall up to a 35-pound bunny with a price tag of $200!

CENTRAL OHIO FIRE MUSEUM & LEARNING CENTER

Address: 260 N. Fourth Street, Columbus, OH 43215

Phone: (614) 464-4099

Website: www.centralohiofiremuseum.com

Hours: Tuesday–Saturday: 10 a.m.–4 p.m.

Cost: $6 Adults
            $4 Children
            $5 Seniors
            Call ahead for group tours and rates

Ages: 3 and up

Stroller and wheelchair friendly: Yes

Length of visit: 1–2 hours

Description and comments:

The Central Ohio Fire Museum is housed in a restored fire station originally built in 1908. Several "man-powered" and "horse-powered" fire trucks are on display. In the early days of the firehouse, the horses lived in the station with the firefighters and you can step through the original stalls that housed them. The stall doors have dents remaining from the horses' hooves. A guide leads you through the museum, explaining the equipment and the history of firefighting and of the station. You will hear the ringing bell that signals a fire. The museum also contains a children's play area complete with a working fire truck cab. Push the buttons and hear the sirens roar. Slide down a fire pole and try on junior-sized fire gear.

The back of the museum contains a very thorough fire

education center. Your children will practice making a 911 call and witness the devastating results of a fire. One room displays items that have been burned in real fires. Learn about safety in your home and understand the effects of several types of kitchen fires. You will be convinced of the importance of fire safety by visiting a bedroom that has been destroyed by a house fire. After your tour, little firefighters receive a memento to remind them of their visit.

COSI

Address: 333 W. Broad Street, Columbus, OH 43215

Phone: (614) 228-2674
            (888) 819-2674

Website: www.cosi.org

Hours: Wednesday–Saturday: 10 a.m.–5 p.m.
            Sunday: Noon–6 p.m.
            Last Friday of Every Month: 5–9 p.m.

            Closed some holidays. Closed part of
            September for maintenance. Check website
            for schedule.

Cost: Exhibits and Live Shows:
            $17.95 Adults (13–59)
            $12.25 Children (2–12)
            $16.95 Seniors (60+)

            Extreme Screen Movie Theater:
            $7.50 Each film, all ages

            $5 Parking

            Exhibits and live shows are free with
            Cincinnati Museum Center membership.
            Movie tickets require purchase.

Ages: All ages

Stroller and wheelchair friendly: Yes

Length of visit: 2 hours–all day

Description and comments:
    COSI is a science museum that will appeal to everyone

in the family. The acronym stands for Center of Science and Industry, but everyone calls it COSI. The excitement begins as soon as you enter the building. Look above to see a unicycle on a high wire that older kids and adults may want to ride later in your visit. Also in the lobby is the electrostatic generator show where you learn about electricity and see someone's hair stand up straight! When you purchase your admission, be sure to pick up a show schedule so that you can plan your day around the shows you want to see. One of our favorites is Rat Basketball, where you can watch two rats compete against each other putting a ball through a basket. You'll learn about how rats are trained. Also very popular are the shows on the Gadgets Stage. These shows vary seasonally and may include chemistry, dry ice, or explosions.

Exhibits are organized into about ten different areas within the museum. Parents with infants, toddlers, or preschoolers will want to spend some time in Little Kidspace, which was designed for and is restricted to young children kindergarten age or younger. Kids can build with blocks, try out the climbing wall, pretend to drive an ambulance, and play in the water area. In the Farm to Table exhibit, kids explore all the stages of food from farming, to the market, to a playhouse filled with building activities. Older siblings can spend time in the Hang Out room, which has activities especially for them and is monitored so that parents can spend time with the younger children.

Children of all ages are fascinated with learning about the properties of water in the Ocean area. They can balance a ball on a fountain of water and make some waves. They will also have fun exploring the submarine area. The Gadgets exhibit area is another fun place with activities like pulling your own weight with ropes and pulleys, and redirecting a laser beam using mirrors. In the Gadgets Café you can take apart everyday objects to see how they work or do science experiments. Reservations are required; sign up early in the day.

School-age children will enjoy the Space exhibit where they can maneuver a robotic Mars rover, learn about gravity, and engage in interactive computer activities. In the Life exhibit area, kids can learn about gestation, birthing, and aging. Three laboratories within the museum allow visitors to view research on pharmacology, language, and visual processes. The Progress exhibit is a place to learn about the history of innovation with displays on Morse code, the evolution of electricity, and early televisions.

Big Science Park is an outdoor area where you can investigate the sustainable, energy efficient POD Home and use a giant lever to lift a car. WOSU is a working TV & radio studio. There are also many interesting hallway exhibits. One of our favorites is the hot air balloon area. The Extreme Screen is a movie theater with a screen that is 83 feet wide and 7 stories tall. There are two movies shown that alternate every hour. There is an additional fee required for the films.

COSI's website has helpful information including suggested itineraries for different ages, and suggested activities in each exhibit area. The museum has a gift shop as well as a restaurant onsite which is a convenient option for lunch. You are also allowed to carry in a packed lunch and eat in the lunch room. COSI is a great museum and well worth the drive to Columbus. It has a reciprocal agreement with the Cincinnati Museum Center, making it free for Cincinnati Museum Center members.

FRANKLIN PARK CONSERVATORY AND BOTANICAL GARDENS

Address: 1777 E. Broad Street, Columbus, OH 43203

Phone: (614) 715-8000

Website: www.fpconservatory.org

Hours: Daily: 10 a.m.–5 p.m.
             Wednesday, extended hours: 10 a.m.–8 p.m.

Cost: $12 Adults
             $6 Children (3–17)
             Free Children 2 and under
             $9 Seniors

Ages: All ages

Stroller and wheelchair friendly: Yes

Length of visit: 2–3 hours

Description and comments:

Franklin Park Conservatory is similar to Cincinnati's Krohn Conservatory, but is larger and expands its focus to include nature-inspired art along with the botanical collections. The conservatory has a permanent collection of Dale Chihuly artwork, several pieces of which are on display at any given time. A botanical garden surrounds the conservatory, providing both an indoor and outdoor experience.

The conservatory is organized by different types of ecosystems. The large Pacific Island Water Garden is located in the South Conservatory and features exotic flora native to the Pacific Islands. Pretend you are on vacation as you stroll through the palm trees, banana trees, and ferns, and watch the Koi fish swim around the pond. Admire the art pieces displayed among the plants. From mid-March through mid-September, butterflies flutter around the room during the annual *Blooms & Butterflies* exhibition.

The Palm House is an elegant Victorian-style glass greenhouse that was built in 1895. It displays 43 different species of palms from all over the world. The North Conservatory houses three different biomes: the Desert, a Tropical Rainforest, and the Himalayan Mountains. You might be surprised by the diversity of cacti and succulents in the desert. Be sure to visit the resident Macaws in the lush rainforest. The Himalayan Mountain biome provides a seasonal experience as flowers bloom in the spring and summer and deciduous trees change colors in the fall. Kids and adults love the garden railway with figures from fairytales and nursery rhymes.

The Dorothy M. Davis Showhouse changes with the seasons and often has beautiful floral displays. Adjacent to the showhouse are two outdoor rooftop gardens: the Zen Terrace and the Grove. Other outdoor areas include the Bonsai Courtyard and Sculpture Garden.

Something that makes the Franklin Park Conservatory truly unique is the Glassblowing Hot Shop. Watch a skilled artist create intricate glass art. Just drop in during their open hours (weekdays from 11 a.m.–2 p.m. and weekends from Noon–3 p.m.) and watch them work for a half hour or so. Kids and adults find it fascinating to see these items being created. Browse the gift shop for pieces that have been made in the Hot Shop. Glassblowing classes are also offered in the evenings.

After leaving the conservatory, take some time to meander through the large Community Garden Campus, the Grand Mallway, Daylily Gardens, and Trial Gardens. Enjoy a picnic lunch at one of the picnic tables near the main entrance or throughout the park, or stop in the Garden Café inside the conservatory. Head to the Grand Mallway for the best view of Light Raiment II, a colorful show of LED lights that illuminates the Palm House each evening starting at dusk.

FRESHWATER FARMS OF OHIO

Address: 2624 N. U.S. Highway 68, Urbana, OH 43078

Phone: (937) 652-3701
            (800) 634-7434

Website: www.fwfarms.com

Hours: Monday–Saturday: 10 a.m.–6 p.m.
            Closed major holidays

Cost: Free admission
            Trout food is 25 cents

Ages: All ages

Stroller and wheelchair friendly: Yes

Length of visit: 1 hour

Description and comments:

Most people don't think of central Ohio as being the likely location for a fish hatchery, but the small town of Urbana, Ohio boasts the largest indoor fish hatchery in the state. Freshwater Farms of Ohio offers a free self-guided tour of the hatchery and welcomes families with children. Kids who like animal interactions will love this place.

When you arrive, drive to the back of the property and park there for the hatchery tour and animal interactions. Be sure to bring plenty of quarters to purchase food for the Trout Feeding Frenzy. The trout swim calmly around their tank until a handful of food is dropped in and then they go crazy competing for bites of food. Don't be surprised if they splash you. Our kids enjoyed feeding them again and again. A petting tank gives kids and adults the opportunity to pet sturgeon. Another interactive area has toads, salamanders, and turtles. View (but don't touch!) an alligator named Fluffy and some snapping turtles. Other tanks house shrimp, catfish, bass, and other varieties of fish.

The Farm Market is at the front of the property. You can purchase fresh, frozen, or smoked trout. They also carry locally made products including honey, cheese, and maple syrup, and pottery crafted by local artists. Freshwater Farms also sells pond supplies. Look behind the market for tanks of koi and tadpoles which are sure to delight kids.

Freshwater Farms hosts several events throughout the year including the Ohio Fish & Shrimp Festival on the third weekend in September. It's a family-friendly event with games, activities, live music, and, of course, Ohio-raised freshwater shrimp.

HOPEWELL CULTURE
NATIONAL HISTORIC PARK

Address: 16062 State Route 104, Chillicothe, OH 45601

Phone: (740) 774-1126

Website: www.nps.gov/hocu

Hours: Grounds
           Daylight Hours

           Visitor Center
           Daily: 8:30 a.m.–5 p.m.
           Open until 6 p.m. between Memorial Day and
           Labor Day

Cost: Free

Ages: 4 and up

Stroller and wheelchair friendly: Trails are flat, but unpaved

Length of visit: 2–4 hours

Description and comments:

Five groupings of Prehistoric Native American Earthworks covering almost 1,200 acres in Chillicothe comprise the Hopewell Culture National Historic Park. Three of these groupings are currently open to the public. The Visitor Center is located at the Mound City Group, the only fully restored site and the smallest of the five sites. The Visitor Center is typical of other National Park sites and offers an orientation film and a small museum containing artifacts that were excavated from the site. Begin your visit here in order to learn about the mounds and the people who built them. *Mysteries of the Ancient Architects* is a 19-minute film that provides an overview of the Hopewell

Culture and the sites in the park. The museum displays 2000-year-old artifacts including pipes and traded items not found in this area such as obsidian, copper, and shark teeth. An interactive computer kiosk provides more in-depth information for curious minds.

The park offers a free Junior Ranger program for visitors ages 5–12. Not only will kids earn a badge for completing the program, but they will learn more while on their visit. Families are encouraged to complete the required activities together. Guided tours and most of the ranger-led programs are offered only between Memorial Day and Labor Day, and a self-guided interpretive trail is available at any time during the year. The park offers a one-mile nature trail that is flat and kid friendly.

Restrooms are available at the Visitor Center. No vending or concessions are available, so plan to bring a picnic if you will be there at lunch time. Picnic tables are available. After your visit to the Mound City Group, consider viewing either the Seip Earthworks or Hopewell Mound Group. Seip Earthworks contains the second largest known Hopewell burial mound. The Hopewell Mound Group was once owned by Mordecai Hopewell and is the largest of the Hopewell earthworks. Archaeologists named the entire culture after this mound group. Hiking, picnic facilities, and restrooms are available at both.

A calendar on the park's website lists upcoming events. Most programs are held during the summer months, but an annual Discovery Day is held each fall.

THE JOHNNY APPLESEED EDUCATIONAL CENTER & MUSEUM

Address: 579 College Way, Urbana, OH 43078

Phone: (937) 484-1303
           (937) 484-1368

Website: http://www.urbana.edu/resources/
           community/johnny-appleseed.html

Hours: Tuesday–Friday: 10 a.m.–2 p.m.
           Saturday: Noon–4 p.m.

Cost: $3 Adults (13+)
           Free Children 12 and under

Ages: 5 and up

Stroller and wheelchair friendly: Yes

Length of visit: 1 hour

Description and comments:

Only one museum in the world is dedicated to Johnny Appleseed, and it's located just an hour and a half from Cincinnati in Urbana, Ohio. Johnny Appleseed is an American legend who some people may not know was actually a real person named John Chapman. Many preschool and elementary school children learn about him in class. Other children might be familiar with him if they've seen the 1948 Disney short film anthology, *Melody Time*. The Johnny Appleseed song is frequently sung before meals in camps and homes across the country: *The Lord is good to me, and so I thank the Lord, for giving me the things I need, the sun and the rain and the appleseed. The Lord is good to me.* This hidden gem of a museum is located on the campus of Urbana University. Why Urbana? The university was built on land donated by a friend of Johnny Appleseed with Johnny's encouragement.

The museum is very small—just one room, but the exhibits are high quality. Visitors learn about both Johnny Appleseed, the legend, and John Chapman, the real person. An interactive exhibit allows you to listen to different songs about Johnny Appleseed. See Johnny Appleseed's Bible, a cider press, a piece of a tree planted by Johnny Appleseed, and a display of Johnny Appleseed collectibles. Another exhibit allows you to view videos about the last living tree known to be planted by Johnny. An activity table for kids is shaped like an apple slice and has coloring pages, games, and puzzles.

Everything in the museum can be viewed in an hour or less. The museum director is extremely knowledgeable about Johnny Appleseed and will answer any questions you have. This Adventure is ideal to pair with either Freshwater Farms of Ohio or Ohio Caverns.

OHIO CAVERNS

Address: 2210 E. State Route 245, West Liberty, OH 43357

Phone: (937) 465-4017

Website: www.ohiocaverns.com

Hours: April–October
            Daily: 9 a.m.–5 p.m.

            November–March
            Daily: 9 a.m.–4 p.m.
            Closed Thanksgiving and Christmas

Cost: $12–$15 Adults
            $8–$12 Children
            Free Children 4 and under

Ages: 3 and up

Stroller and wheelchair friendly: No, but if a wheelchair is needed, you may call and reserve a wheelchair accessible tour in advance.

Length of visit: 1–3 hours

Description and comments:

Ohio Caverns claims the largest caverns in the state, covering over two miles of passages with depths of 30 to 103 feet. No matter what the season is, the temperature inside the caves at Ohio Caverns is always a constant 54° Fahrenheit. This makes it a perfect Adventure for those hot summer days when you are searching for ways to keep cool.

The two main tours available are the Natural Wonder Tour and the Historic Tour. The Natural Wonder Tour is a one-mile trek through the cave and takes just under an hour. This tour, available year round, explores several rooms including "Fantasyland," "Palace of the Gods," the "Big Room," and other unique features of the cave. The Historic Tour is available only from April through October. It's about ¾ miles and lasts about 45 minutes. The Historic Tour explores the original entrance and parts of the caverns that were toured by visitors after it was first discovered in 1897. A short bus ride takes visitors to the beginning of this tour. A shorter Limestone Tour is also available by reservation only. It's about ¼ miles and last 25 minutes.

Inside the caves are a variety of formations: stalactites, stalagmites, columns, soda straws, and fossils. Many of these formations inside the caverns are still active and growing. Ohio Caverns is nicknamed one of "America's most colorful caverns." The minerals found in the cavern produce many different colors including yellow, orange, red, purple, blue, and black. Tours of the caverns boast sights of formations such as Crystal King, a stalactite that measures almost five feet long, and the Old Town Pump, which is a column that resembles a small hand pump. Some people think the Old Town Pump resembles a horse more than a pump. Take a look and see what you think!

Ohio Caverns has modern restroom facilities and a large parking lot. After your tour, save some time to play on the playground, enjoy a picnic lunch under the shelter, or mine for gems. Purchase a bag of mining "rough" in the gift shop and take it outside to the giant wooden sluice. Using the screens provided, sift through the rough. You might find a gemstone, minerals, fossils, or an arrowhead. The bags have been seeded so that you won't be disappointed.

The paths in the caverns are level and easy to walk, but strollers are too wide to navigate the narrow passageways. If you are in need of a wheelchair accessible tour, be sure to call in advance to schedule a tour.

OHIO STATEHOUSE

Address: 1 Capitol Square, Columbus, OH 43215

Phone: (614) 728-2695

Website: www.ohiostatehouse.org/tours

Hours: Statehouse
               Monday–Friday: 7 a.m.–6 p.m.
               Saturday–Sunday: 11 a.m.–5 p.m.

               Tours
               Monday–Friday: 10 a.m.–3 p.m.
               Saturday–Sunday: Noon–3 p.m.
               Tours depart on the hour

Cost: Free
               Hourly charges for parking garage

Ages: 9 and up

Stroller and wheelchair friendly: Yes

Length of visit: 1–3 hours

Description and comments:

See your tax dollars hard at work when you tour the Ohio Statehouse. Both self-guided tours and guided tours are offered. Groups of ten or more are asked to schedule tours at least a week in advance. The most convenient parking is in the garage under the Statehouse. Enter the building at the Third Street entrance.

For self-guided tours, start in the Map Room and pick up a tour brochure or try out the audio wand tours (hand held device with tour audio), or podcast tours (www. ohiostatehouse.org/tours/IpodPodcastTours.aspx).   Most areas of the Statehouse have free WiFi, making it easier to access the podcasts. All tours are free. You will be asked to leave your driver's license in exchange for an audio wand.

Guided tours depart at the top of each hour. Arrive in the Map Room about five minutes before the tour begins. The floor of this aptly named room contains a map showing each county in the state of Ohio. The map is made out of five types of marble and limestone. Your tour guide will explain the Greek Revival architecture of the impressive structure, take you into several areas of the Capitol, and share anecdotes about the history of the building and the work that goes on within its walls. On your tour you'll see the spectacular Rotunda with its 29-foot wide skylight at the top and 5,000 hand-cut pieces of marble creating the floor under your feet. The tour takes you to the Atrium, where President Abraham Lincoln stood and addressed a group of about 1,500 people. Then, enter either the chambers of the Ohio Senate or the House of Representatives (rooms are nearly identical). Be sure to save time for the Statehouse Museum. The museum is for all ages and is filled with interactive and hands-on activities and displays. Learn how legislators serve, how they are elected, and the roles they play in government. Follow a bill turning into a law through the 3D chronology and be educated on past Ohio governors.

Take a walk on the lawn of Capitol Square and view statues of famous historical figures like Christopher Columbus, former Ohio presidents, and soldiers serving in our country's wars. If the weather is nice, pack your lunch and enjoy it on the lawn. A café is also available inside the Capitol for meals or snacks.

SERPENT MOUND

<u>Address:</u>   3850 State Route 73, Peebles, OH 45660

<u>Phone:</u>   (937) 386-6025
             (800) 752-2757

<u>Website:</u>   www.ohiohistory.org/serpentmound

<u>Hours:</u>   Park Grounds
           Daily: daylight hours

           Museum
           Open Seasonally
           Check website for details

<u>Cost:</u>   Free admission
           $7 Parking
           Check for AAA discount

<u>Ages:</u>   3 and up

<u>Stroller and wheelchair friendly:</u> Yes

<u>Length of visit:</u> 1 hour

<u>Description and comments:</u>

Serpent Mound is one of the earthworks built by prehistoric Native Americans. In the shape of a coiled serpent, the earthwork is about three feet high and over 1,300 feet long. It is believed to have been built by the Fort Ancient culture, although there are Adena burial mounds located nearby. The purpose of the mound is unknown, but it has been determined that it was not used for burial and that the head is aligned to the sunset of the summer solstice. Visitors are not permitted to climb on the mound, but can walk on a paved path around it. Climb the 35-foot tower for a better view of the serpent design. The grounds also include a wigwam model and a Native American garden planted with corn, beans, squash, and gourds.

Additionally, the park includes a museum. One exhibit explores different theories about the meaning of the design. A model shows how the Adena burial mounds were constructed. A timeline shows all the prehistoric cultures of Ohio, and artifacts associated with each culture are displayed. Another exhibit is about the geology of the area.

THE TOPIARY PARK

Address: 480 E. Town Street, Columbus, OH 43215

Phone: (614) 645-0197

Website: www.topiarypark.org

Hours: Park Grounds:
            Daylight hours, year round
            Best viewing: April–November

            Visitor's Center:
            April through mid–November
            Tuesday and Thursday: 11 a.m.–3 p.m.
            Saturday: 11 a.m.–4 p.m.
            Sunday: Noon–4 p.m.

Cost: Free

Ages: All

Stroller and wheelchair friendly: Yes

Length of visit: 1 hour

Description and comments:

The Topiary Park, in downtown Columbus, is perhaps the most unique attraction in this book. The theme of the garden is a famous post-impressionist painting by Georges Seurat, *A Sunday on the Island of La Grande Jatte*. This painting is well known for its use of pointillism. We applaud the creative mind that dreamed up the idea to recreate a painting using shrubbery. It is truly one of a kind. All of the figures in the painting have been recreated in topiary form, including 54 people, eight boats, three dogs, a monkey, and a cat. Kids get a kick out of seeing people and animals carved from shrubs. They can walk up to them, around them, and view them from all sides. Touching and climbing are not permitted. Even the river in the painting was recreated by installing a pond in the park. A bronze plaque on one of the paths marks the point where you stand to view the figures as they appear in the painting. The painting does not include a cat and it is not visible from the plaque, but was added to the park as a fun touch. Challenge your children to find it. For some additional fun, visit the website and look for the education packet. It includes an outline drawing of the painting that you can print and have your kids color. Other educational materials are also included. The park includes benches and picnic facilities. This is a delightful spot to have a picnic lunch after visiting another attraction in Columbus. The visitor's center is open seasonally and includes a gift shop. Check the website for information on scheduling a docent-led tour of the park. Restrooms are open daily.

INDIANA

THE CHILDREN'S MUSEUM OF INDIANAPOLIS

Address: 3000 N. Meridian Street, Indianapolis, IN 46208

Phone: (317) 334-3322

Website: www.childrensmuseum.org

Hours: March–Labor Day
Daily: 10 a.m.–5 p.m.

Labor Day–February
Tuesday–Sunday: 10 a.m.–5 p.m.
Closed some holidays

Cost: $18.50 Adults
$13.50 Children (2–17)
Free Children 1 and under, with
accompanying adult
$17.50 Seniors (60+)

Occasional free days and evenings; check
website for details.

Free Parking in garage

The Children's Museum of Indianapolis does
not have a reciprocal agreement with
Cincinnati Museum Center.

Ages: All ages

Stroller and wheelchair friendly: Yes

Length of visit: 2–6 hours

Description and comments:

The Indianapolis Children's Museum is the world's
biggest children's museum and houses an impressive

collection of 11 major galleries exploring the physical and natural sciences, history, world cultures, and the arts. Dinosphere might be a favorite spot for junior paleontologists. Walk among the dinosaurs, dig up fossils, and listen to a thunderstorm roll in above you. A working turn-of-the-century carousel delights the young and the old alike. Climb aboard and experience the sights and sounds of the magical merry-go-round for an additional $1 fee. An 1868, 35-foot long steam engine is at the center of the All Aboard train exhibit. Guests can view both real and model trains in this area while exploring what life was like in the glory days of the locomotive. Playscape welcomes visitors ages five and younger (with their parents) where they can play, build, pretend, and splash. Walking up the ramp in the center of the building you can't miss the brilliant, 43-foot tall, Dale Chihuly glass sculpture, *Fireworks of Glass*. This amazing centerpiece will fascinate children and adults of every age. Other exhibits in the museum include an Egyptian tomb, a planetarium, Flight Adventures, a hands-on science gallery, a biotechnology learning area, and Health House — a place where kids learn about making healthy choices. Discover what makes Anne Frank, Ruby Bridges, and Ryan White important figures in 20th century history and explore how children can make a difference in the world around them. Visit the Lilly Theater for wonderful live plays with professional actors (included with museum admission) designed for children of all ages. The museum's website includes more information on activities and galleries most suitable for each age group.

At the end of the day, gather at the top of the ramp for a parade. Each child will receive a flag to carry and they will march happily out of the museum. What a great way to end the day!

CONNER PRAIRIE INTERACTIVE
HISTORY PARK

Address: 13400 Allisonville Road, Fishers, IN 46038

Phone: (800) 966-1836

Website: www.connerprairie.org

Hours: May–October
            Tuesday–Sunday: 10 a.m.–5 p.m.

            November–March
            Thursday–Sunday: 10 a.m.–3 p.m.

            April
            Thursday–Sunday: 10 a.m.–5 p.m.

            Outdoor experiences are open approximately
            April–October.
            Indoor experience areas are open year round.
            Closed Thanksgiving, Christmas Eve,
            Christmas Day, and New Year's Day

Cost: April–October (see website for specific dates)
            $15 Adults
            $10 Children (2-12)
            Free Children under 2
            $14 Seniors (65+)
            $15 Balloon Ride (Adults and Children)

            November–March (see website for specific
            dates)
            $6 Adults
            $6 Children (2-12)
            Free Children under 2

            Military and group discounts are offered

Ages: 3 and up

Stroller and wheelchair friendly: Yes

Length of visit: 4 hours–all day

Description and comments:

Are you a history buff? Do you think it's easier to understand history by experiencing it rather than only reading about historical events? Then Conner Prairie is the place for you! Conner Prairie is a Smithsonian-affiliated living history museum just north of Indianapolis. When you walk through the gates, you are immersed in time periods from 1816 through the days of the Civil War. Find costumed interpreters throughout the park who portray historically accurate but fictional characters from each time period. Spend the day experiencing history with authentic characters from the past.

The bulk of Conner Prairie consists of five distinct outdoor experiences. The first of these areas is the 1859 Balloon Voyage. Ascend 350 feet into the air in the amazing hot air balloon. Hold on tight and enjoy the view as you soar high above Conner Prairie. Interactive displays explore the science of balloon travel and early aviation.

Next, explore the 1816 Lenape Indian Village. Learn how to throw a tomahawk, listen to stories of these Native Americans, and explore the village trading post. A former chief of the Lenape Indian tribe is on site to share stories and information with visitors.

The Conner Homestead is the third stop on the grounds. Visit historic buildings including the original home of William Conner and interact with farm animals like sheep, goats, hogs, and cows in the Animal Encounters Barn. These animals are historic breeds from the 1800's, some of which are also on the list of endangered animals. Animal specialists are on hand to explain more about preserving these breeds.

Allow plenty of time to explore 1836 Prairietown. Meet the residents of the town and ask questions about anything relating to their daily life as it existed in the 19th century. The residents of the town portray their 1836 characters quite convincingly. It's worth the time to read about each citizen of Prairietown on the website before visiting. The descriptions of the characters will help explain the dynamics taking place between the citizens and might help stimulate questions. (Listen closely and you'll hear how the townspeople feel about Dr. Campbell.) When arriving in Prairietown, stop at the Outfitter's Cart and spin the wheel to determine your trade or skill for the day. Kids have the chance to earn money in the town by asking residents for chores or by completing the tasks on their cards. Money they earn can be used in the store to purchase small 1836 goodies like marbles and hair bows. Parents will be happy to know that the entire village is filled with historical reproductions so kids are free to touch and explore anything they see. Adventure Guidebooks are also available which provide challenging scenarios for older kids to solve. For those five and under, ask for a Seek and Find Guidebook to use while exploring the town. Check the daily schedule on the reverse side of the map for story times, craft activities, and demonstrations.

The final area is 1863 Civil War Journey: Raid on Indiana. Here you will find a unique, lifelike interactive experience depicting a southern Indiana town following a raid by Confederate General John Hunt Morgan. Meet the authentic local residents and learn the roles they played during the Civil War. Visit a soldier's camp, participate in military drills, and enjoy shows using technology and special effects including loud noises and strobe lights. Because of the intense themes and images of war, this area is recommended for children fourth grade and older. A Civil War themed play area containing a climbable steamboat and water play area is available for those who are too young for this experience.

Conner Prairie also has year-round indoor experiences. Inside the Welcome Center find an exhibit area called "Create.Connect" that explores pioneer science as it relates to today. Try your hand at building a Rube Goldberg Machine™ (a machine that requires a complex process to perform a simple task), designing and testing a windmill, or experimenting with simple circuits. Create prairie crafts in the Craft Corner, and visit Discovery Zone, a miniature town perfect for kids six and under. While in this tiny town, shop in the market, milk a cow, and purchase a ticket for the train. Plenty of couches are available for parents while the kids play.

For lunch options, either pack a picnic or eat at the Café on the Common. If you are packing a picnic, there are picnic tables and shaded areas outside the welcome center and near the café. In September and October visit the Apple Store containing lots of delicious apple treats.

Conner Prairie is wheelchair and stroller accessible. Large wheeled strollers are best for navigating the gravel pathways and bumpy roads. See website for more specific accessibility information.

NCAA HALL OF CHAMPIONS

Address: 700 W. Washington Street, Indianapolis, IN
46204

Phone: (317) 917-6084

Website: www.ncaahallofchampions.org

Hours: Tuesday–Saturday: 10 a.m.–5 p.m.
Sunday: Noon–5 p.m.
Home football game days: 10 a.m.–3 p.m.

Cost: $5 Adults
$3 Children (6–18)
Free Children 5 and under
$3 Seniors (60+)

Ages: 5 and up

Stroller and wheelchair friendly: Yes

Length of visit: 2 hours

Description and comments:

Calling all sports fans! We found the museum for you. The NCAA Hall of Champions is dedicated to representing all 23 National Collegiate Athletic Association sports with informative and interactive exhibits.

The first floor of the museum includes displays for each of the 23 different NCAA sports. Of course you are familiar with basketball, football, and baseball, but did you know that fencing, bowling, and rowing are also included in the lineup of NCAA sports? Look for a map highlighting locations of each NCAA school and play a game of mascot mix-up. Current year championship banners for each sport are on display along with a Hall of Fame highlighting award winners of the past. Interactive trivia stations displayed with each sport test your knowledge of the rules and history of the games.

The second floor is packed with interactive displays that will keep everyone busy and quite possibly tire them out, too! Shoot some hoops in the 1930's retro basketball gymnasium; try your hand at simulated sports like soccer, hockey, and golf; put your feet in the starting blocks on the track; and measure your vertical leap. Stand in front of a window protecting you from a tennis ball flying at 75 mph and try not to flinch. Take a break in the Media Room and watch sporting broadcasts and news on the television screens.

The museum is located in White River State Park in the heart of downtown Indianapolis. Several more unique attractions also call this park home including the Indianapolis Zoo, IMAX Theater, Indiana State Museum, Indiana History Center, Congressional Medal of Honor Memorial, Victory Field (home of the Indianapolis Indians), and Eiteljorg Museum of American Indians and Western Art. The park itself covers 250 acres and includes green space, gardens, trails, trees, and waterways. The White River flows through the park as does Historic Central Canal. A quaint Canal Walk lined with restaurants, apartments, and store fronts follows along the waterway. For some extra exercise, paddleboats, surreys, and bicycles are available to rent along the canal from www.wheelfunrentals.com. For more information on White River State Park including special events, concert series, festivals, and more, head to www. inwhiteriver.com.

THE VIRGINIA B. FAIRBANKS ART & NATURE PARK: 100 ACRES

Address: 4000 Michigan Road, Indianapolis, IN 46208

Phone: (317) 923-1331

Website: www.imamuseum.org/visit/100acres

Hours: Daily: Dawn–Dusk

Cost: Free

Ages: All ages

Stroller and wheelchair friendly: Yes

Length of visit: 2–4 hours

Description and comments:

On the grounds of the Indianapolis Museum of Art is the Virginia B. Fairbanks Art & Nature Park: 100 Acres. This is one unique park! The park contains many features typically seen in a park including wetlands, woodlands, a meadow, and a lake. Several trails lead visitors through the different terrains of the park exposing them to many varied plant and animal species.

The quirky and creative artworks displayed throughout the park are what make 100 Acres so special. From the parking lot, you see *Free Basket*, which is a series of blue and red steel arcs which resemble the trajectory of a bouncing basketball. Of course, there are basketball goals on the sculpture too, making it a fun place to take a few shots. Tip: Bring your own basketball to be able to fully enjoy *Free Basket*.

Other artwork includes a much larger-than-life skeleton emerging from the ground. *Funky Bones* is a group of 20 fiberglass pieces with depictions of bones on each one, combining together to form a creative skeleton. The "bones" beg for kids to climb and jump between the pieces. Take a walk to the lake to see *Eden II* where a mysterious boat appears to be stranded near the shore. Also in the lake is *Indy Isle*, a man-made island resembling an igloo, which is fully inhabitable. *Chop Stick* is a sculpture created from a fallen 100-foot-tall tulip tree and provides seating, swings, and tables to enjoy. *Bench Around the Lake* is a series of 15 creatively designed yellow benches bordering the bank of the White River. Challenge yourself to find all of these playful and unusual benches.

In all, 12 unique works of art reside on the grounds of 100 Acres. This is an outstanding place to walk, think, explore, and play. Pack a picnic and enjoy your lunch on a blanket in the meadow. The unconventional artwork makes this an interesting place to create unforgettable memories while exploring nature in a new way.

Outside of 100 Acres are another 152 acres of gardens and grounds to explore. The Oldfields-Lilly House & Gardens is a National Historic Landmark and located within the museum grounds. It is a historic house museum that has been restored to its 1930's décor. Of course you can also venture into the Indianapolis Art Museum and explore the artwork housed inside. Before your visit ends, make sure to take your picture in front of the iconic LOVE sculpture in front of the museum.

KENTUCKY

AMERICAN SADDLEBRED MUSEUM

Address: 4083 Iron Works Parkway, Lexington, KY 40511

Phone: (859) 259-2746

Website: www.asbmuseum.org

Hours: Memorial Day–Labor Day
             Daily: 9 a.m.–6 p.m.

             September–May
             Daily: 9 a.m.–5 p.m.

             Closed on Mondays and Tuesdays,
             November–March

             Closed some holidays

Cost: Includes admission to the Kentucky Horse Park

             Mid-March–October 31
             $16 Adults
             $8 Children (7–12)
             Free Children 6 and under
             $15 Seniors (65+)
             $3 Parking

             November 1–mid-March
             $9 Adults
             $6 Children (7–12)
             Free Children 6 and under
             $8 Seniors (65+)
             Free Parking

Ages: 3 and up

Stroller and wheelchair friendly: Yes

Length of visit: 1 hour

Description and comments:

Don't miss seeing the American Saddlebred Museum on your visit to the Kentucky Horse Park. The museum is located on the grounds of the Kentucky Horse Park and is included in the admission price. The museum is home to the largest collection of Saddlebred artifacts in the world. See award winning movies and learn about the role that the Saddlebred horse has played in the history of America. There are many interactive, one-of-a-kind displays for kids. It also houses a large library and a gift shop. This is a fun stop that pairs perfectly with the Kentucky Horse Park.

BELLE OF LOUISVILLE

<u>Address:</u>   401 W. River Road, Louisville, KY 40202
         Parking lot is located at 131 W. River Road

<u>Phone:</u>   (502) 574-2992
         (866) 832-0011

<u>Website:</u>   www.belleoflouisville.com

<u>Hours:</u>   Varies by season; check website for schedule

<u>Cost:</u>   Sightseeing cruises
         $21 Adults
         $12 Children (3–12)
         Free Children 2 and Under, but ticket is
         required
         $20 Seniors (60+)
         Check website for prices on lunch, dinner, and
         themed cruises

<u>Ages:</u>   All ages

<u>Stroller and wheelchair friendly:</u> Yes

<u>Length of visit:</u> Most cruises last 2 hours; boarding begins
         30 minutes prior to departure

<u>Description and comments:</u>

   The *Belle of Louisville* is a beautiful, historic riverboat and holds the distinction of being the oldest operating Mississippi River-style steamboat in the world.   This 100-year-old boat was originally named the *Idlewild* and was built in Pittsburgh, Pennsylvania in 1914.   Driven entirely by a large, red paddlewheel, the Belle offers sightseeing, lunch, and dinner cruises. Lunch and dinner cruises require advance reservations, but tickets for sightseeing cruises can usually be purchased just prior to boarding. Meals are served buffet-style with reserved seating. Narration is provided during the meal, highlighting points of interest along the Ohio River. Saturday afternoons are family cruises and include family-friendly entertainment such as a clown or magician. Sunday cruises feature music and perhaps a few games if there are plenty of kids on board. Our tweens and teens found it far more entertaining than they anticipated. On Fridays, the education coordinator is typically aboard and offers narration about the history of the steamboat. Sightseeing cruises are conducted at the same time as dining cruises, but the sightseeing passengers are restricted to the upper deck until the meal is complete. Sightseeing cruise passengers can enjoy the view during the meal and then participate in games and activities afterwards.

Cruises on the *Belle of Louisville* are typically scheduled for Thursday through Sunday. Her sister ship, the *Spirit of Jefferson*, offers several more cruises, including weekday cruises and a one-hour Harbor History tour on Saturdays. Both boats offer themed cruises for various holidays and seasons. Check their website for the cruise schedule.

Consider combining your cruise with a visit to Louisville's beautiful Waterfront Park. It offers wet and dry playgrounds as well as a pedestrian bridge that crosses the river, and has many scheduled events. Check the event schedule at www.louisvillewaterfrontpark.com for more information.

EVERGREEN HILLS MAZE

Address: Cemetery Street, Flemingsburg, KY 41041
           Adjacent to Fleming County Cemetery

Phone: (606) 782-1459

Hours: September–October
           Saturday: 10 a.m.–5 p.m.
           Sunday: 1–5 p.m.
           Closed during inclement weather.
           Other times available by appointment for
           groups of 6 or more. Night treks are available.

Cost: $6 Children and adults

Ages: 6 and up

Stroller and wheelchair friendly: No

Length of visit: 1–2 hours

Description and comments:

Imagine getting lost in the woods on purpose. Most people are probably familiar with a corn maze. Now picture a corn maze, but bigger, and on hilly terrain. The Pine Tree Maze is composed of 12,000 Eastern White Pine trees planted in 1995. These 30 foot trees form approximately 300 rooms and cover 15 acres. Walking through this family-friendly maze will take most people about 45 minutes. The maze can be enjoyed just as a puzzle of nature while listening to birds and walking in the shade. Add to the difficulty of the maze by playing Murder in the Maze. The game takes about two hours and involves looking for seven signs throughout the maze which contain clues to uncover the mystery. The night treks are an exciting way to get lost in the dark and are perfect for teenagers.

Charlotte's Web is another maze on the property. It is small and deceptively difficult. Designed by a mathematician, it consists of circles with only one way in and one way out. See if you have what it takes to complete this challenging maze. A large Grass Labyrinth is also available to explore.

Cookouts can be arranged and picnic tables are available. A portable toilet is available during September and October.

FRAZIER HISTORY MUSEUM

Address: 829 W. Main Street, Louisville, KY 40404

Phone: (502) 753-5663

Website: www.fraziermuseum.org

Hours: Monday–Saturday: 9 a.m.–5 p.m.
Sunday: Noon–5 p.m.
Closed: Easter, Thanksgiving, Christmas Day

Cost: $18.50 Adults
$14.50 Students (14–17 & college with ID)
$10 Children (5–13)
Free   Children 4 and under
$16.50 Seniors and Military
$10 Teachers

Ages: 8 and up

Stroller and wheelchair friendly: Yes

Length of visit: 2–4 hours

Description and comments:

Located in downtown Louisville, the Frazier History Museum is filled with knights, princesses, toy soldiers, and more. It is part of "Museum Row on Main," which is a collection of nine museums and attractions all located within a four block area in Louisville.

The Frazier History Museum is home to the Royal Armouries, a collection of armor and armaments that were formerly housed in the Tower of London. It is the largest collection of European armor outside of Europe. The museum is also host to one of the largest public displays of toy soldiers in the United States. The toy soldier collection includes over 10,000 pieces representing soldiers from Ancient Egypt, the Ottoman Empire, South Africa, India, Europe, and North and South America.

The museum takes visitors through over 1000 years of history with displays from The Bronze Age through the early 20ᵗʰ Century. Start your exploration of the museum on the third floor, where the displays from the earliest time periods are found. Find out about interesting historical characters such as Joan of Arc, Annie Oakley, Geronimo, and Lewis & Clark. You will also discover information about many historical events including the Black Death, the Hundred Years War, the Pony Express, the Texas Revolution, and the Civil War. The museum is proud to hold the nation's oldest surviving Civil War monument, located in the museum entrance. You'll find artifacts throughout the museum such as Daniel Boone's Bible, George Washington's rifle, Teddy Roosevelt's "Big Stick" used on his African safari, and Jesse James' revolver. In all, there are over 5000 artifacts representing stories in the history of our world.

The museum offers live sword fighting demonstrations and costumed interpreters featuring historical accounts by characters including Buffalo Bill, Abraham Lincoln, Catherine the Great, Vikings, and many others. Visit their website for a schedule of daily performances.

Interactive exhibits include a dress-up area for children, touchable armor, and an area to experience the strength required to shoot a bow and arrow. The museum is currently planning a renovation which will result in a larger Civil War display and include more interactive exhibits.

KENTUCKY DERBY MUSEUM

Address: 704 Central Avenue, Louisville, KY 40208

Phone: (502) 637-7097

Website: www.derbymuseum.org

Hours: March 15–November 30
           Monday–Saturday: 8 a.m.–5 p.m.
           Sunday: 11 a.m.–5 p.m.

           December 1–March 14
           Monday–Saturday: 9 a.m.–5 p.m.
           Sunday: 11 a.m.–5 p.m.

Cost: $14 Adults
           $11 Young Adults (13–18)
           $6 Children (5–12)
           Free Children under 5
           $13 Seniors (55+)

           AAA, Military, Group, and School discounts
           offered

Ages: 5 and up

Stroller and wheelchair friendly: Yes

Length of visit: 2–4 hours

Description and comments:

   What is the oldest continuous sporting event in the
United States? It's the Kentucky Derby! You can experience
the horses, the jockeys, the fancy hats, and everything the
Derby has to offer when you visit this family-friendly
museum located on the grounds of the famous racetrack
with the twin spires.

The Kentucky Derby Museum underwent a renovation in 2010 adding many interactive features. The first floor of the museum highlights parts of the Derby having to do with the fan experience, while the upstairs looks into the lives of the horses.

On the first floor, see both elegant and eccentric hats and outfits worn to the festivities, view a 360° movie called *The Greatest Race* about the Derby, the horses, and the trainers, and take your picture with the current year's Derby winner and jockey. View footage of past races, listen to interviews with race participants, and read about different experiences of race day from a variety of perspectives. Learn how to place a bet through an entertaining interactive display, then watch the race, scan your ticket, and discover your (imaginary) winnings. Mount a model of a horse, try to maintain a jockey's stance, and watch your horse advance on the video monitor as you race your friends. Try your hand in the broadcast booth by attempting to call your own race karaoke style.

On the second floor, experience the life of a Thoroughbred through all stages of the horse's life. Exhibits explain racehorses' lives beginning with the day they are born. Look into life on the farm, the physical characteristics of a winning horse, and the difficulty of winning this prestigious race. Take a glimpse into the life of a jockey and appreciate the amount of athleticism that is required for this profession. Try on the jockey silks, then step into the starting gates, mount your horse and say, "Cheese."

Included with general museum admission is the Historic Walking Tour. This tour lasts 30 minutes and takes you into Churchill Downs. Sit in the grandstand and hear several stories and facts about the race.

The Barn & Backside Tour is available for an additional charge. (See website for details on this and other special tour options.) It is recommended that this hour-long tour be booked in advance. Board the tour bus and take a ride to the far side of the track and see the stables, trainers, and horses. You might have a chance to watch horses being bathed, led to the track, and, if you're lucky, you may see them training, too. For those hoping to catch the horses in action, the early morning hours are your best chance. This is a great tour for horse lovers to see more of Churchill Downs from a different perspective. This tour is not wheelchair or stroller friendly and is best for children 8 and up.

KENTUCKY GATEWAY MUSEUM CENTER

Address: 215 Sutton Street, Maysville, KY 41056

Phone: (606) 564-5865

Website: www.kygmc.org

Hours: Tuesday–Friday: 10 a.m.–4 p.m.
Saturday: 10 a.m.–3 p.m.

Cost: $10 Adults
$2 Students (6 and up)
Free Children 5 and under

Ages: 5 and up

Stroller and wheelchair friendly: Yes

Length of visit: 1–2 hours

Description and comments:

Maysville, Kentucky, with a population of 9,000 people is a small city, but it boasts an impressive museum that matches its significant history. Located upriver from Cincinnati, about an hour-and-15-minute drive, Maysville was settled by frontiersmen including Daniel Boone and Simon Kenton. The city was an important stop on the Underground Railroad. In 1833, Harriet Beecher Stowe visited and watched a slave auction which she later described in her novel *Uncle Tom's Cabin*. The Kentucky Gateway Museum Center contains a Regional History Museum to showcase the area's abundant history. Dioramas, fine art, and a diverse collection of artifacts including commonplace objects from furniture to weapons tell the story of the people who shaped Maysville and the surrounding region.

Our favorite part of the museum center is the

internationally acclaimed KSB Miniatures Collection. The 3,300-square-foot gallery is filled with miniature houses and vignettes with rotating displays. All of the miniatures are made to a 1/12ᵗʰ scale and the intricate details inspire awe. Many of the pieces recreate historic buildings, such as a 15ᵗʰ century English pub or 19ᵗʰ century Maysville church. The most impressive of these is Spencer House, the palace of Princess Diana's ancestors. Other miniatures portray scenes from stories like *The Hobbit*, nursery rhymes, or fairytales. While kids are fascinated by the collection, parents should be aware that there are no hands-on exhibits in this gallery.

A third section of the Kentucky Gateway Museum Center features changing exhibits. The fourth section is an extensive Research Library with materials on both history and genealogy. The institution began as a public library in 1878, and the collection includes original documents dating back to the 1700's, along with original maps and other primary sources for researchers. The Museum Shop sells a wide collection of books about the region including photography books, biographies, and cookbooks, as well as other unique merchandise.

While in Maysville, don't miss the Maysville Floodwall Murals (25 E. McDonald Parkway), created by Robert Dafford, the same artist who painted the Roebling Murals in Covington (see page 75). If you're looking for a sweet ending to your Adventure before heading back to Cincinnati, drive out to Magee's Bakery (8188 Orangeburg Road) for some Transparent Pie.

KENTUCKY HORSE PARK

<u>Address:</u>   4089 Iron Works Parkway, Lexington, KY 40511

<u>Phone:</u>   (859) 233-4304
            (800) 678-8813

<u>Website:</u>   www.kyhorsepark.com

<u>Hours:</u>   Mid-March–October
            Daily: 9 a.m.–5 p.m.

            November–mid-March
            Wednesday–Sunday: 9 a.m.–5 p.m.

<u>Cost:</u>   Includes admission to the American
            Saddlebred Museum
            General Admission includes next day free

            Mid-March–October
            $16 Adults
            $8 Children (7–12)
            Free Children 6 and under
            $15 Seniors (62+)
            $3 Parking

            November–mid-March
            $10 Adults
            $5 Children (7–12)
            Free Children 6 and under
            $9 Seniors (62+)
            Free Parking

            There is an extra fee for pony rides, horseback
            rides, and farm tours. Check the website for
            more information.

            Check for AAA discount.

<u>Ages:</u>   3 and up

<u>Stroller and wheelchair friendly:</u> Yes

<u>Length of visit:</u> 3–6 hours

<u>Description and comments:</u>

If you have a horse lover in your family, or if you are interested in the pastime that has made Kentucky famous, then the Kentucky Horse Park is worth the trip. This is a hands-on park and living museum. It is situated on a stunning campus in the rolling hills of Kentucky. Younger kids (under 90 pounds) can take a pony ride; while the older kids (at least 7 years old and 4 feet tall) may venture on a 45-minute trail ride (both for an additional fee). See a wide range of shows including the Parade of Breeds. In this program you will see some of the 35 breeds in the park and learn what makes each of them unique. The handlers are handsome in authentic clothing as would have been worn in different parts of the world. After the show there is time to visit the horses and talk to their handlers.

See a Mare and Foal show where the babies and moms are displayed together. Another performance will explain how to take care of a horse and give some audience members a chance to participate in some of these tasks.

See the Draft Horses being groomed and prepared for their day of work pulling the trolleys. Later take the free ten-minute narrated trolley ride highlighting the different areas of the park.

In the Hall of Champions, you will see many former award-winning race horses that now make their home at the Kentucky Horse Park. View clips of their races and snap some close up pictures as the horses are paraded past the audience. Notice the tombstones of the former stars of the park in the Legends of the Park. The burial place of the Legendary Man O' War is marked by a majestic bronze sculpture.

If you are visiting with children, be sure to visit the Kids Barn filled with educational, interactive, and fun activities for kids 13 and younger. Help groom horses, go on scavenger hunts, and say hello to the horses in the barn. Kids love the Champion's Arena where they can try out the miniature jumping course just for them (no horses required). The Kids Barn also has daily presentations, check the website for the schedule.

Next, venture indoors to the International Museum of the Horse. This museum "is committed to educating the general public, equestrian and academic communities about the relationship between man and the horse throughout history and the world." In its 38,000 square feet you will take a historical journey of the horse throughout time. Your kids will recognize many well known lessons straight from their history books in the displays. The Kentucky Horse Park also has two free movies explaining the relationships between horses and people. There is food available for purchase inside the park. If you pack a lunch, bring a blanket and enjoy a picnic on the grounds outside of the park.

KENTUCKY SCIENCE CENTER

Address: 727 W. Main Street, Louisville, KY 40202

Phone: (502) 561-6100

Website: www.kysciencecenter.org

Hours: Sunday–Thursday: 9:30 a.m.–5 p.m.
Friday–Saturday: 9:30 a.m.–9 p.m.

Cost: $13 Adults
$11 Children (2–12)
Free admission to permanent exhibits for
Cincinnati Museum Center members

$7 per person film tickets (Adults and children)
Combination ticket prices available for exhibits
and film tickets

$5 admission after 5 p.m. on Fridays and
Saturdays

Ages: All ages

Stroller and wheelchair friendly: Yes

Length of visit: 3 hours–all day

Description and comments:

With three floors of educational fun, the Kentucky
Science Center is a big hit with kids and their parents. The
museum covers a wide range of sciences including physical,
biological, and earth sciences, and has plenty of hands-on
learning as well as interesting shows to watch.

The first floor has a large temporary exhibit space as well
as the KidZone designed especially for children ages 7 and
under. KidZone contains climbing structures, puzzles, and

science experiments. It also houses a rocket ship, a school bus, and an ambulance for some imaginative play. The Baby Crater is an area in KidZone specifically for non-walkers. One fun feature is a song titled *Tra La La Boom De Ay* that plays with the push of a button in the kid-sized restrooms, complete with lyrics posted on the wall; the entire tune is devoted to kids using the potty.

The second floor was the favorite spot for our kids. An exhibit area called The World We Create focuses on physical science and has many hands-on exhibits. Interact with wind tunnels, pneumatic conveyors, gears, a light table, and more. Kids who are avid builders won't be disappointed. The World Around Us focuses on earth science. Sit in front of a green screen, pretend to be your favorite meteorologist, and watch your forecast on a TV. Learn about animals, ecology, recycling, and more.

The World Within Us is a tasteful exhibit on biological science on the third floor, but deserves a note about several mature content areas. They are located throughout the third floor and most are marked with signs. One exhibit focuses on the various systems in the body, including the respiratory, digestive, immune, and reproductive systems. Kids learn about the immune system by playing a video game with T cells, B cells, and macrophages. An exhibit called Amazing Beginning features fetuses at different gestational ages. Other exhibits explore birth control and substance abuse. A driving simulator helps kids understand the difference between driving sober and driving drunk.

A four-story large-format theater offers various films at different times during the day. When you enter the museum, make note of the times along with the show times

for the Explosion of the Day and Story Times. A Subway®
restaurant is located on site and is a convenient option for
lunch.

LOUISVILLE MEGA CAVERN

Address: 1841 Taylor Avenue, Louisville, KY 40213

Phone: (877) 614-6342

Website: www.louisvillemegacavern.com

Hours: Historic Tram Tours
           Daily: January–October
           Tours leave on the hour; hours vary by season;
           check website or call

           Arrive 15-20 minutes prior to scheduled tour
           time

           MEGA Zips
           Monday–Friday: 9 a.m.–5 p.m.
           Saturday–Sunday: 9 a.m.–10 p.m.
           By appointment; hours may vary slightly
           (closed Christmas Day)
           Arrive 45 minutes prior to scheduled tour time

           MEGA Quest
           Daily (closed Christmas Day)
           Three hour sessions start at 9 a.m., Noon, and 3
           p.m.

           Arrive 15-20 minutes prior to scheduled tour
           time

           Lights Under Louisville
           Mid-November–New Year's Day (Open
           Christmas Day)
           Monday–Friday: 6–10 p.m.
           Saturday and Sunday: 5–10 p.m.

<u>Cost:</u>   Historic Tram Tours
              $13.50 Adults
              $8 Children (3–11)
              Free Children 2 and under
              $12 Seniors

              MEGA Zips
              $59 Early Bird–available for tours at 9 a.m. and
              10 a.m. on weekdays only
              $69 Weekdays
              $79 Weekends
              Adults and children pay the same price

              MEGA Quest
              $35 Adults
              $29 Children (5–11)

              Lights Under Louisville
              $25 per car, truck, SUV, or minivan

<u>Ages:</u>   Historic Tram Tours: 5 and up
              MEGA Zips: 8 and up
              MEGA Quest: 5 and up
              Lights Under Louisville: all ages

Stroller and wheelchair friendly: Historic Tram Tour and
Lights Under Louisville only

Length of visit: Historic Tram Tour: 1–2 hours
                  MEGA Zips: 2 hours
                  MEGA Quest: 3 hours
                  Lights Under Louisville: <1 hour

Description and comments:

Louisville MEGA Cavern is a former mine that has been
converted into a rather unconventional business park. The
100-acre cavern was mined for limestone from the 1930's to

the 1970's, creating 17 miles of passages. During the Cold War it was equipped to be a nuclear fallout shelter. Now it houses a variety of businesses from RV storage to a recycling facility to the world's only underground zip lining course. At Christmas time, the cavern is adorned with sparkling lights, making it the world's only underground holiday light show. Does that sound like an interesting cavern? Then consider taking the Historic Tram Tour to learn more.

The Historic Tram Tour lasts a little over an hour and is narrated by an entertaining guide. During the tour visitors learn the history and many interesting facts about the cavern. Although the cavern was a mine, not a cave, it is wet and has begun to form stalactites and stalagmites. During the tour, a short film about the Cold War is shown, and then the tram drives past a life-size diorama depicting the cavern as a nuclear fallout shelter. The tour is geared for all ages, but if you have preschool aged children, keep in mind that the cavern is dark and the guides may joke about ghosts.

There's only one place in the world with underground zip lines and that's Louisville MEGA Zips. It's a great twist for experienced zip liners, but also suitable for first-timers. Be sure to make an advance reservation because group sizes are limited to 12 people. The tour starts in an equipment room where everyone is outfitted with a full harness and a hard hat with a headlamp. They thoughtfully include a pouch to safely hold your camera or smartphone. Other belongings can be stowed in a locked trunk until the end of the tour. The course includes six zip lines and two rope bridges. The first zip line is the Bunny Zip, a short line to help overcome any fears before progressing to the longer and faster lines in darker passages. The final line is a dual line where participants can race each other. The guides are knowledgeable and entertaining and ensure that everyone stays safe. Our kids loved the experience, especially when the guides encouraged them to let go of the handle bar and go cannonball style on one of the lines.

At the time of writing this, the MEGA Quest ropes course was newly opened and offers three-hour sessions. This area is suitable for ages 5 and up and includes swinging ropes and wooden bridges, cargo nets, tunnels, and also a zip line. Participants choose between an easy, medium, or hard path through the course. Safety harnesses of the highest quality are used. The area is available for overnight lock-ins for youth groups.

LOUISVILLE SLUGGER MUSEUM & FACTORY

Address: 800 W. Main Street, Louisville, KY 40202

Phone: (877) 775-8443

Website: www.sluggermuseum.org

Hours: Monday–Saturday: 9 a.m.–5 p.m.
            Sunday: 11 a.m.–5 p.m.
            Check website for extended summer hours
            and holiday closings

Cost: $12 Adults (13–59)
            $7 Children (6–12)
            Free Children 5 and under
            $11 Seniors (60+)

            There is an extra charge for the batting cages.
            ($1 for 10 balls)

Ages: 3 and up

Stroller and wheelchair friendly: Yes

Length of visit: 2 hours for museum visit; 25 minutes for
factory tour

Description and comments:

You'll be certain you've found the Louisville Slugger
Museum & Factory when you catch sight of The World's
Biggest Bat leaning against the side of the building. This bat
was constructed with the exact, scaled dimensions of Babe
Ruth's bat. Inside the building is an oversized sculpture of
a baseball glove. Take the stairs to the second floor and snap
a picture of your kids in the monstrous mitt.

When you arrive, purchase your ticket for the museum

and factory tour. You will receive a ticket for the next available tour. While you are waiting for your tour to begin, run the bases of the field while listening to the sounds of famous plays being called. You can also practice your swing in Bud's Batting Cage. Check for the starting times of the movie *The Heart of the Game* and be sure to fit this into your schedule.

The tour takes you through the factory where the bats are produced. (Bat production currently takes place seven days a week.) Smell the sawdust while watching the precision methods for crafting the bats to the exact specifications of each player. Talk to the employees at each step of production and see how these Louisville Slugger bats are made. At the end of the tour, each person will receive a miniature bat as a memento of their visit.

The museum was renovated in 2009 and added many displays. New exhibits include a display featuring a Babe Ruth bat. Babe carved a notch in this bat for each home run hit with it. There is a new interactive area with memorabilia of some of baseball's unforgettable moments. Also included is a hands-on display of bats used by professional ball players. A Joe DiMaggio bat (never before on display) is now available for visitors to see. There is also a children's activity area included in the museum.

In the gift shop you can order a personalized bat with either your name or your signature on it. They also carry Louisville Slugger walking canes and many other souvenirs.

OLD FORT HARROD STATE PARK

Address: 100 S. College Street, Harrodsburg, KY 40330

Phone: (859) 734-3314

Website: www.parks.ky.gov/parks/recreationparks/
fort-harrod/

Hours: Grounds
Daily: 8 a.m.–Dusk

Fort and Lincoln Marriage Temple
March–November
Wednesday–Saturday: 9 a.m.–5 p.m.
Sunday: Noon–5 p.m.

December–February
Monday–Friday: 8 a.m.–4:30 p.m.

Cost: Free admission to park

Fort
$5 Adults
$3 Children (6–12)
Free Children 5 and under

Ages: 3 and up

Stroller and wheelchair friendly: Partially

Length of visit: 2–4 hours

Description and comments:

Old Fort Harrod State Park is the home of a replica fort built by Kentucky Pioneer James Harrod in 1774. This fort became the first permanent settlement in Kentucky. Although the fort is the official focal point of the park, a giant Osage Orange tree rivals it in popularity among kids.

A split trunk makes it extremely appealing for kids to climb on. Some branches rest on the ground while others ascend quite high. The tree is a gathering place for locals and the site of weekly summer concerts. Musicians perform under the shade of the tree while kids scale the tree and parents watch from picnic tables and folding chairs.

The self-guided fort tour is a must for families. Learn about life as a pioneer in this living history museum. Costumed interpreters abound throughout the fort, performing many different demonstrations. Visit the Blacksmith Shed and watch the blacksmith at work. He might even use your kids as apprentices and let them operate the bellows. See women operating spinning wheels, sewing, making soap (available in the gift shop), and performing other household tasks. Tour the block houses and learn how the pioneers defended themselves against Native American attacks. Visit the tiny schoolhouse and imagine how the lives of pioneer children were different from students today. Kids love the sheep pen in the middle of the fort. Purchase a bag of food in the gift shop then feed the sheep. This is a fun and engaging way to learn history.

Other features in the park include a federal monument to George Rogers Clark and a pioneer cemetery where the first white child in Kentucky is buried. The Lincoln Marriage Temple shelters the log cabin where Abraham Lincoln's parents were married.

While in Harrodsburg, consider a stop at the Kentucky Fudge Company (225 South Main Street). This eatery is housed in the historic Dedman Drug Store, circa 1865. The building that once housed a pharmacy and soda fountain has come full circle and once again is a place where people can meet for ice cream, fudge, or a meal.

SHAKER VILLAGE OF PLEASANT HILL

Address: 3501 Lexington Road, Harrodsburg, KY 40330

Phone: (800) 734-5611

Website: www.shakervillageky.org

Hours: April–October
                 Daily: 10 a.m.–5 p.m.

                 November–March
                 Daily: 10 a.m.–4 p.m.

Cost: April–October
                 $15 Adults
                 $5 Children (6–12)
                 Free Children 5 and under, with paying adult

                 November–March
                 $7 Adults
                 $3 Children (6–12)
                 Free Children 5 and under, with paying adult

Ages: 4 and up

Stroller and wheelchair friendly: Partially

Length of visit: All day–2 days

Description and comments:

You'll feel like you've stepped into another era when you arrive at the Shaker Village of Pleasant Hill, a beautiful historic restoration surrounded by a 3,000-acre nature preserve. You could easily spend two days exploring everything they have to offer, so if you only have one day, plan your time wisely. Pick up the daily schedule when you arrive and take note of activities that are offered only once a day.

Start your tour of the village at the Centre Family Dwelling which has been converted into a living history museum. Here you'll learn about the history and practices of the Shakers, a religious sect that arrived in America in 1774 and established the Pleasant Hill village in the early 1800's. Costumed interpreters demonstrate various chores and crafts such as spinning, weaving, and broom making. Your kids may even have the opportunity to help. Visit the schoolroom where young visitors can dress up in Shaker attire and write on slates with chalk.

Be sure to attend one of the scheduled music programs in the Meeting House. An interpreter discusses the customs of the Shakers, sings several Shaker Hymns, and then teaches willing participants a Shaker song and dance. Farm activities are popular with kids. Help gather eggs in the morning, watch the farm hands harness the horses for their work day, visit the animals, and meander through the gardens. The employees at the village are enthusiastic and willing to answer whatever questions you have.

For a special treat, enjoy lunch or dinner at The Trustees' Office Dining Room which serves Shaker recipes and seasonal Kentucky dishes prepared with vegetables grown in the village garden. Don't miss the delicious Shaker Lemon Pie. Reservations are recommended for all meals. While in the Trustees' Office, admire the elegant design of the pair of spiral staircases for which Shakers are well known.

A short drive from the village, Shaker Landing is home to the *Dixie Belle* Riverboat. A one-hour narrated cruise provides scenic views of the Kentucky River Palisades and High Bridge, which was the tallest bridge in the world when it was built in 1877. The captain points out wildlife along the way.

While you can easily visit the Shaker Village of Pleasant Hill and return to Cincinnati in a single day, if you are able to spend the night in the Inn at Shaker Village, it greatly enhances the experience. Sleep in one of the original, 200-year-old Shaker buildings which are furnished with reproduction Shaker beds, chairs, and dressers. Spend a leisurely evening exploring the grounds and trails through the nature preserve.

TOYOTA VISITOR CENTER AND PLANT TOUR

Address: 1001 Cherry Blossom Way, Georgetown, KY
            40324

Phone: (502) 868-3027
            (800) TMM-4485

Website: www.toyotageorgetown.com/tour.asp

Hours: Visitor Center
            Monday–Friday: 9 a.m.–4 p.m.

            Plant Tours
            Monday–Friday: 10 a.m., Noon, 2 p.m.
            Thursday: 6 p.m.

Cost: Free

Ages: First grade and older for family tours
            Fourth grade and older for group tours

Stroller and wheelchair friendly: Wheelchair accessible

Length of visit: 2 hours

Description and comments:

It might surprise you that the second largest Toyota plant in the world is located just an hour and a half from Cincinnati in Georgetown, Kentucky. It is also the largest Toyota plant in North America and offers tours to visitors. Approximately 7,000 employees produce around 2,000 vehicles per day, including the Camry, Avalon, and Venza models, as well as their hybrid counterparts.

While walk-ins are accommodated if there is availability, advance reservations for a Plant Tour are strongly recommended. When you arrive at the plant, be sure to lock purses and other bags in the trunk of your vehicle as these items are prohibited inside. Phones and cameras are permitted inside the Visitor Center, but not on the Plant Tour. Visitor Center personnel are happy to hold these items for you during the tour. Explore the exhibits while waiting for your tour to begin. Displays provide an overview of the manufacturing process as well as information about Toyota's environmental protection practices and community involvement. The very first Camry produced in the plant in 1988 is exhibited. Take a close-up look at the latest Camry, Avalon, and Venza models. Kids love to sit behind the wheel and pretend to drive.

Plant Tour participants ride on a tram and wear headphones in order to better hear the tour guide in the noisy factory. Visitors see the entire process from stamping the metal that becomes the car body to the addition of the many parts and finishing touches. Some tasks, such as spot welding, are performed by robots. Kids are fascinated by the robotic carts navigating their way through the plant carrying parts. During the hour-and-a-half-long tour, see the steps vehicles go through over the course of about the 20 hours it requires to build a car. Kids and adults find this glimpse into the inner workings of an automobile manufacturing plant both entertaining and educational.

Part Three

PLANNING HELP

PLANNING YOUR OWN ADVENTURES

This section is designed to help you plan your own adventures. We have provided some sample itineraries to get you off to a quick start, for both summer and year-round schedules. Following the itineraries, our Adventure Table contains an alphabetical list of all the Adventures in table format, clearly showing which activities fit into each category and location. Use this list to find Adventures suitable for your family. Take special note of our free attractions to help you manage the cost of your Adventures.

SAMPLE ITINERARIES:

Summer 1:
Gorman Heritage Farm
Findlay Market
Heritage Village Museum at Sharon Woods
Cox Arboretum MetroPark
Warren County History Center
Rumpke Landfill Tour
Conner Prairie Interactive History Park
William Howard Taft National Historic Site
Vent Haven Museum

Summer 2:
Carillon Historical Park
Loveland Castle-Chateau LaRoche
Roebling Murals
Winton Woods
Fort Ancient Earthworks and Nature Preserve

Hueston Woods State Park
Fountain Square
Reds Hall of Fame and Museum
Kentucky Horse Park
Boonshoft Museum of Discovery

Year-Round 1:

January - American Sign Museum
February - St. Mary's Cathedral Basilica of the Assumption
March - Garden of Hope
April - Paul Brown Stadium Tour
May - Jane's Saddlebag
June - Glen Helen Nature Preserve and Raptor Center
July - Wegerzyn Gardens MetroPark
August - Ohio Caverns
September - Apple Picking
October - Evergreen Hills Maze
November - Tower A at Cincinnati Union Terminal
December - Clifton Mill

Year-Round 2:

January - National Museum of the United States Air Force
February - Warren County History Center and Glendower
March - Cincinnati Nature Center - Rowe Woods
April - Trammel Fossil Park
May - Little Miami Bike Trail
June - Sawyer Point Park and Yeatman's Cove
July - Parky's Wet Playground
August - Fernald Preserve
September - Young's Jersey Dairy
October - Clifton Gorge
November - Carew Tower
December - Behringer -Crawford Museum

SEASONAL ADVENTURES AND OTHER RECOMMENDATIONS

In case you are looking for some other tried and true adventure locations, here are some seasonal Adventures and other activities you might be interested in exploring. We've compiled these lists together with our friends and readers.

Parks and Playgrounds

Alms Park
www.cincinnatiparks.com/index.php/alms-park

Ault Park
www.cincinnatiparks.com/index.php/ault-park

Eden Park
www.cincinnatiparks.com/index.php/eden-park

Lincoln Woods
www.boonecountyky.org/parks/ParkInfo/9

Lunken Airport Playfield (page 58)

Megaland at Colerain Park (page 149)

Nisbet Park, Loveland Karl Brown Way at the Little Miami Bike Trail

Sawyer Point (page 77)

Theodore M. Berry International Friendship Park
www.cincinnatiparks.com/index.php/friendship-park

Washington Park
www.cincinnatiparks.com/index.php/washington-park

Wet Playgrounds

Clippard Park
www.colerain.org/department/public-services/parks-services/ township-parks/clippard-park/

Home of the Brave Park
www.symmestownship.org/departments/parks-recreation/parks/ home-of-the-brave-park.aspx

Parky's Wet Playgrounds (page 158)

Pleasant Ridge Sprayground
pleasantridge.org/living-in-the-ridge/pool-sprayground-park

Smale Riverfront Park
www.cincinnatiparks.com/index.php/smale-riverfront-park

Washington Park
www.cincinnatiparks.com/index.php/washington-park

U-Pick Farms

A&M Farm Orchard
www.aandmfarm.blogspot.com

Barker's Blackberry Hill Winery
www.kyagr.com/KDAPage.aspx?id=3318

Blooms & Berries
www.bloomsandberries.com

Gorman Heritage Farm
www.gormanfarm.org/product/flowers/

Irons Fruit Farm
www.ironsfruitfarm.com

Rouster's Apple House
www.sites.google.com/site/roustersapplehouse

Stokes Berry Farm
www.stokesberryfarm.com

Fall Adventures

Blooms & Berries
www.bloomsandberries.com

Bonnybrook Farms
www.bonnybrookfarms.com

Brown's Family Farm Market
www.brownsfarmmarket.com

Burger Farm & Garden Center
www.burgerfarms.com

Hidden Valley Fruit Farm
www.hiddenvalleyfruitfarm.com

Kings Island
www.visitkingsisland.com

Kinman Farms
www.kinmanfarmsfallfest.com

Niederman Family Farm
www.niedermanfamilyfarm.com

Parky's Farm Halloween Nights (page 156)

Shaw Farms
www.shawfarms.com

Windmill Farm Market
www.windmillfarmmarket.com

Christmas Adventures

Christmas at the Galt House Hotel in Louisville
www.christmasatthegalthouse.com

The Christmas Ranch
www.thechristmasranch.com

Cincinnati Museum Center Holiday Junction
www.cincymuseum.org/holiday

Cincinnati Zoo Festival of Lights
cincinnatizoo.org/events/festival-of-lights/

Clifton Mill Legendary Lights (page 192)

Creation Museum Christmas Town
www.creationmuseum.org

Krohn Conservatory Holiday Floral Show
www.cincinnatiparks.com/krohn

Loveland United Methodist Church Living Nativity
www.lovelandumc.org

Pyramid Hill Holiday Lights on the Hill
www.pyramidhill.org

Sharon Woods Holiday in Lights and Santaland
www.holidayinlights.com

Performances

Calico Children's Theatre
www.ucclermont.edu/community_arts/calico_theatre.html

Children's Theatre of Cincinnati
www.thechildrenstheatre.com

Cincinnati Symphony Orchestra Lollipops Family Concerts
www.cincinnatisymphony.org

Circus Mojo
www.circusmojo.com

La Comedia Dinner Theatre
www.lacomedia.com

Madcap Puppets
www.madcappuppets.com

The Magic of Phil Dalton
www.phildalton.com

Peanut Butter and Jam Sessions
www.lintonmusic.org/peanut-butter-and-jam-series

Shakespeare in the Park
www.cincyshakes.com

ADVENTURE	Page #	Animals	Archaeology	Art	Dinosaurs	Free
American Girl® Boutique and Bistro	213					
American Legacy Tours	22					
American Saddlebred Museum	252	x				
American Sign Museum	24			x		
Anderson Ferry	96					
Anthony-Thomas Chocolate Factory	216					
BB Riverboats	26					
The Beach Waterpark	98					
Behringer-Crawford Museum	28		x			
Belle of Louisville	254					
Big Bone Lick State Historic Site	100	x	x			x
Boonshoft Museum of Discovery	184	x	x			
Carew Tower Observation Deck	30					
Carillon Historical Park	186					
Carriage Hill Metro Park	188	x				x
Central Ohio Fire Museum & Learning Center	218					
The Children's Museum of Indianapolis	241		x	x	x	
Chilo Lock 34 Park	102					x
Cincinnati Art Museum	32			x		•
Cincinnati History Museum at Cincinnati Museum Center	34					
Cincinnati Nature Center - Rowe Woods	104	x				
Cincinnati/Northern Kentucky International Airport	106					x
Cincinnati Observatory	37					
Cincinnati Reds Hall of Fame & Museum	39					
Cincinnati Zoo & Botanical Garden	41	x				

Gardens	History	Museums	Outdoor	Planes	Play Areas	Preschoolers	Tours	Trains	Transportation	Walking/Hiking	Central Cincinnati	Greater Cincinnati	Dayton	Ohio	Indiana	Kentucky
						x								x		
	x		x				x			x	x			x		
	x	x														x
	x	x					x				x			x		
	x		x						x			x		x		x
							x							x		
			x			x	x		x		x					x
			x		x	x						x		x		
x	x	x			x	x		x	x		x					x
	x		x				x	x								x
	x	x	x							x		x				x
	x	x			x	x							x	x		
	x		x								x			x		
	x	x	x	x		x		x	x				x	x		
x	x	x	x		x	x				x			x	x		
	x	x			x	x	x							x		
	x	x			x	x		x							x	
	x	x	x		x	x			x			x		x		
		x									x			x		
	x	x				x			x		x			x		
x			x		x	x					x		x	x		
			x				x	x				x				x
	x		x				x				x			x		
	x	x			x						x			x		
x			x			x		x			x				x	

ADVENTURE	Page #	Animals	Archaeology	Art	Dinosaurs	Free
Clifton Gorge State Nature Preserve	190					x
Clifton Mill	192					
CoCo Key Water Resort	108					
Coney Island	110					
Conner Prairie Interactive History Park	243	x				
COSI	220					
Cox Arboretum MetroPark	194					x
Creation Museum	112	x	x		x	
Crooked Run Nature Preserve	114	x				x
The Dayton Art Institute	196			x		
Dayton Aviation Heritage National Historic Park	198					x
Duke Energy Children's Museum at Cincinnati Museum Center	43	x				
EnterTRAINment Junction	115					
Evergreen Hills Maze	256					
Fernald Preserve	117					x
Fire Museum of Greater Cincinnati	48					
Findlay Market	46					x
Fort Ancient Earthworks and Nature Preserve	119		x			
Fountain Square	50					•
Franklin Park Conservatory and Botanical Gardens	223			x		
Frazier History Museum	258			x		
Freshwater Farms of Ohio	226	x				x
Garden of Hope	52			x		•
Glen Helen Nature Preserve and Raptor Center	200	x				•
Gorman Heritage Farm	121	x				
Grant Boyhood Home and Schoolhouse	123					

Gardens	History	Museums	Outdoor	Planes	Play Areas	Preschoolers	Tours	Trains	Transportation	Walking/Hiking	Central Cincinnati	Greater Cincinnati	Dayton	Ohio	Indiana	Kentucky
			X							X			X	X		
	X						X						X	X		
					X	X						X		X		
			X		X	X						X		X		
	X	X	X		X	X			X						X	
	X	X			X	X								X		
X			X			X							X	X		
X	X	X	X									X				X
		X	X			X				X		X		X		
		X				X							X	X		
	X	X		X						X			X	X		
		X			X	X					X			X		
	X	X			X	X	X	X				X		X		
			X							X						X
X	X	X	X							X				X		
	X	X				X					X			X		
	X		X								X				X	
	X	X	X		X					X		X		X		
	X		X								X			X		
X		X	X											X		
	X	X														X
						X								X		
X			X				X				X			X		
			X							X			X	X		
X	X		X			X				X		X		X		
X	X					X						X		X		

Gardens	History	Museums	Outdoor	Planes	Play Areas	Preschoolers	Tours	Trains	Transportation	Walking/Hiking	Central Cincinnati	Greater Cincinnati	Dayton	Ohio	Indiana	Kentucky
	x	x					x					x		x		
												x		x		
	x	x	x		•	•	x					x		x		
x			x		x	x		x		x		x		x		
		x	x							x				x		
			x			x				x		x		x		
	x		x		x	x						x				x
	x	x												x		
					x	x						x		x		
	x	x					x									x
	x	x														x
	x	x	x		x	x										x
		x			x	x										x
			x		x	x		x				x		x		
x											x			x		
			x		x	x						x		x		
					x			x	x			x		x		
			x							x		x		x		
							x									x
	x	x				x										x
x	x		x			x						x		x		
			x		x	x				x	x			x		
			x				x							x		
			x		x	x				x		x		x		
	x		x				x		x	x		x		x		
		x	x		x	x				x		x		x		

Gardens	History	Museums	Outdoor	Planes	Play Areas	Preschoolers	Tours	Trains	Transportation	Walking/Hiking	Central Cincinnati	Greater Cincinnati	Dayton	Ohio	Indiana	Kentucky
x	x			x	x						x			x		
	x	x	x						x				x	x		
	x	x									x			x		
	x	x													x	
											x			x		
					x	x					x					x
					x	x				x				x		
x	x	x						x						x		
	x	x	x													x
					x	x						x		x		
		x			x	x						x		x		
		x			x	x						x		x		
						x					x			x		
		x							x	x	x			x		x
x		x	x								x	x		x		
	x		x									x				x
	x	x	x				x	x			x					x
	x		x		x	x			x		x			x		x
											x			x		
	x		x								x			x		
			x				x					x		x		
	x		x		x	x				x	x			x		
			x							x				x		x

ADVENTURE	Page #	Animals	Archaeology	Art	Dinosaurs	Free
Shaker Village of Pleasant Hill	279	x				
Sharon Woods	166					•
Sky Galley Restaurant at Lunken Airport	79					
St. Mary's Cathedral Basilica of the Assumption	80			x		•
Sunrock Farm	82	x				
SunWatch Indian Village / Archaeological Park	204		x			
The Topiary Park	238			x		x
Totter's Otterville	83				x	
Tower A at Cincinnati Union Terminal	84					x
Toyota Visitor Center and Plant Tour	282					x
Trammel Fossil Park	168		x			x
Tri-State Warbird Museum	169					
Unmuseum at the Contemporary Arts Center	86			x		•
Vent Haven Museum	88					
The Virginia B. Fairbanks Art & Nature Park: 100 Acres	249			x		x
Warren County History Center and Glendower	171					
Wegerzyn Gardens MetroPark	206					x
William Howard Taft National Historic Site	90					x
Winton Woods	173	x				•
Wolf Creek Habitat	175	x				•
Woodland Mound	177					•
World Peace Bell	92					x
World's Largest Horseshoe Crab	179	x				x
Young's Jersey Dairy	208	x				

• *See individual listings for parking fees, restricted days, and specific cost information.*

Gardens	History	Museums	Outdoor	Planes	Play Areas	Preschoolers	Tours	Trains	Transportation	Walking/Hiking	Central Cincinnati	Greater Cincinnati	Dayton	Ohio	Indiana	Kentucky
	X	X	X							X						X
		X	X		X	X				X		X		X		
				X		X			X		X			X		
							X				X					X
			X			X	X				X					X
	X	X	X			X							X	X		
X			X			X								X		
		X			X	X					X					X
	X	X				X		X	X		X			X		
							X		X							X
		X				X						X		X		
	X	X		X					X			X				
		X				X					X			X		
	X	X					X				X					X
X			X		X	X				X					X	
	X	X										X		X		
X			X		X	X				X			X	X		
	X	X					X				X			X		
			X		X	X				X		X		X		
			X									X			X	
			X		X	X				X		X		X		
			X								X					X
X			X			X						X		X		
			X		X	X							X	X		

We'd love to hear your comments, questions, suggestions, and adventure stories. If you know about a location that isn't in the book but should be, please let us know. We love to speak to groups and we'd be happy to talk to you about scheduling a visit. Please contact us for more information.

Facebook: Adventures Around Cincinnati
Twitter: AdventureCincy
Email: ContactUs@AdventuresAroundCincinnati.com
Pinterest: AdventureCincy
Google+:   Adventures Around Cincinnati

Enjoy your Adventures!

ABOUT THE AUTHORS

Laura Hoevener married her husband John in 1994. Together they have three children, Daniel (Age 14), Anna (Age 11), and Morgan (Age 4). Laura moved to the Cincinnati area in 1999 after living in Michigan, Indiana, and Wisconsin, and now lives in Miami Township in Clermont County. She has an engineering degree from the University of Wisconsin and has worked in the manufacturing and utilities industries. She is currently a professional mom who homeschools her kids and is active in her church. She has as much fun finding new things to do and exploring the area as her kids do, and she's always on the lookout for new and interesting adventures.

Terri Weeks is a mom to Connor (age 15), Corinne (age 13), and Camille (age 11) and has been married to her husband Curtis since 1993. Terri is a graduate of Purdue University and worked as a mechanical engineer before becoming a stay-at-home mom, then a travel writer. Originally from Pittsburgh, she now resides in Miami Township in Clermont County. She loves to travel and explore new places with her family, and enjoys encouraging other families to travel. She also writes a travel blog called Travel50StatesWithKids. com which is based on her family's goal to visit all 50 states by the time her kids graduate from high school. She is a member of the Midwest Travel Writers Association.